**W9-ABP-240**

**Hypothesis
and Evidence in
Psychoanalysis**

# Hypothesis and Evidence in Psychoanalysis

Marshall Edelson

**The University of Chicago Press**

*Chicago and London*

The University of Chicago Press, Chicago 60637
The University of Chicago Press, Ltd., London

Library of Congress Cataloging in Publication Data

Edelson, Marshall, 1928–
    Hypothesis and evidence in psychoanalysis.

    Bibliography: p.
    Includes index.
    1. Psychoanalysis.  2. Hypothesis.  3. Evidence.
I. Title [DNLM: 1. Psychoanalytic theory. 2. Psycho-
analysis. WM 460 E2lh]
BF175.E29      1984        616.89'17        83-9281
ISBN 0-226-18432-3

MARSHALL EDELSON is professor of psychiatry at the
Yale University School of Medicine, director of education in the Yale Department of Psychiatry, and director
of research in the Outpatient Division of the Connecti-
cut Mental Health Center. Dr. Edelson has both a
Ph.D. and an M.D. and is a certified, practicing psychoanalyst. His books include *The Termination of Intensive Psychotherapy* (1963); *Ego Psychology, Group
Dynamics and the Therapeutic Community* (1964);
*Sociotherapy and Psychotherapy* (1970); *The Practice
of Sociotherapy: A Case Study* (1970); *The Idea of a
Mental Illness* (1971); *Language and Interpretation in
Psychoanalysis* (1975).

For my mother Ida

# Contents

# Acknowledgments

Jonathan Edelson has been for me over a number of years in actuality and in my mind's eye an unwavering, encouraging, responsive, and keenly insightful reader. He alone has read every version of the manuscript as it evolved, and, himself immersed in studies of the philosophy of science, he has commented throughout substantively and instructively upon it. Once, when I expressed doubts about what audience such a book might have, he said, as I remember, "Don't write it for your generation. Write it for mine." His contribution to me as well as to the work is incalculable.

Lottie M. Newman in an especially useful discussion helped me to articulate just why and for whom I was writing this book. Donald Spence gave the near-final manuscript a careful reading, which stimulated me to revise and polish. James Blight, Lester Luborsky, Ken Marcus, and Richard Newman also read the near-final manuscript, and each raised thoughtful questions and made useful suggestions. Their enthusiastic reaction to and confidence in the book meant a lot to me, as did the strength of Albert Solnit's sense of its importance to a future generation of psychoanalysts.

Morton F. Reiser, professor and chairman of the Department of Psychiatry at Yale University, and currently the president of the American Psychoanalytic Association, has been an important mentor and colleague. He has provided me with more kinds of support than he is aware of, not the least of which comes from his sharing my conviction that the future of psychoanalysis as a scientific discipline requires energetic, even urgent, attention to the mitigation of obstacles to clinical research in general and single subject clinical research in particular. He is an exemplar of the coexistence of far-ranging scientific interests: he has a deep commitment to furthering developments in the neural sciences, is dedicated to the practice of clinical psychoanalysis, and has a lively appreciation of the exciting phenomena to be found in the psychoanalytic situation.

Rebecca, David, and Zelda, while disavowing any interest in the content of what I was writing, showed a friendly and gratifyingly persistent interest that I write; they regularly urged me to get on with it. Zelda, as through the years, has lovingly held things together.

Amy Rock has been indefatigable, good-humored, and intelligent in carrying out the task of typing and retyping numerous drafts.

I was supported in part by NIMH Psychiatric Education Research grant no. MH-15096, while writing this book.

Portions of Chapters 3, 8, 9, 10, and 11 in this book appeared as a paper entitled "Is Testing Psychoanalytic Hypotheses in the Psychoanalytic Situation Really Impossible?" in *The Psychoanalytic Study of the Child* (1983), 38:61–109. I am grateful to the Yale University Press for their permission to use this material here also.

# Introduction

Is there empirical evidence that provides support, acceptable by scientific canons, for the claim that psychoanalysis as treatment is efficacious? Is there empirical evidence that justifies, according to scientific canons, provisional acceptance of psychoanalytic hypotheses about neurotic symptoms, dreams, and parapraxes as true over rival hypotheses? In our society, threatened as it is by endemic irrationality and swept by anti-intellectual currents, those who are especially concerned to preserve, to put forward, and indeed to insist upon adherence to cognitive scientific canons increasingly and ever more emphatically, it seems to me, answer these two questions "No." More seriously, that negative answer has come to include the assertion "and it is in principle impossible to obtain such evidence by psychoanalytic methods of investigation."

Psychoanalysts cannot remain mute before such an answer to these questions. They cannot dismissively belittle those who make it. They cannot evade it by taking refuge in redefining psychoanalysis as a branch of the humanities—a hermeneutic discipline seeking only to detect and explicate in a singular instance the multitude of possible meanings that what an analysand reports may have for him.[1]

This redefinition usually seems to imply rejection of a view of psychoanalysis as a science. For if psychoanalysis were to be so viewed, like any other science it would perforce have to conform in its reasoning and methods to scientific canons. These canons presuppose a search for general statements about the actual (and not merely some possible) world, which are objectively true of it, in the sense that what they assert corresponds to something in that actual world.[2] The canons define what

1. The pronouns "he," "him," and "his" refer throughout to a person of either gender, unless the context indicates otherwise.
2. "Objectively" here does not imply science excludes interest in subjective phenomena. Subjective phenomena like irrational phenomena are part of the actual world, which

standards must be met by a particular kind of reasoning—the reasoning which leads to a conclusion that provisional acceptance of the truth of an assertion about the actual world is or is not justified in the light of empirical evidence. These canons also define what methods for obtaining this evidence are required if such reasoning is to meet these standards.

How remain mute, as policymakers in our society must decide in what way to distribute finite available resources among competing ends, and among competing means for achieving the same end? How evade, as patients must decide, among literally hundreds of treatments competing for their scarce resources, on the fastest, least costly treatment— but also on the treatment that will do the particular job the patient wants done and in the way the patient wants to do it? Will dismissive belittling attract to psychoanalysis a new generation of scientists, scholars, and physicians, who are appropriately skeptical as they must decide how to allocate their intellectual commitments and career aspirations among competing disciplines and competing activities within a discipline?

Ordinarily, it would seem enough that a practicing clinician should possess those conceptual tools just sufficient to enable him to evaluate the rival hypotheses, and the rival practical proposals, with which he is confronted in the literature of his own field. It is not usually expected that he should also take an interest in the esoterica of, much less prove himself to have expert knowledge in, the philosophy of science. That seems to be as it should be.

However, I do not believe that now psychoanalysts can remain complacently confident that, no matter how psychoanalysis responds to its challengers, it will continue to be regarded as a useful method of investigation and a credible body of knowledge; patients will continue to present themselves as prospective analysands; and new generations of clinicians will continue to want to learn how to carry out psychoanalysis as a treatment.

I am a practicing psychoanalyst. Like my colleagues, I observe and indeed am immersed in the clinical data in question. I participate, with whatever skills I have, in a process which in the psychoanalytic situation produces such data. I not only study and teach psychoanalytic theory but also use it in that situation.

Yet in this book I do not generate a new psychoanalytic hypothesis,

is as it is independent of our theoretical attempts to approximate it and our descriptions or knowledge of it. The fact that phenomena are subjective or irrational should not be confused with the fact that we may choose to study such phenomena objectively or rationally.

argue for one psychoanalytic hypothesis against another, or present the rich clinical examples for which another psychoanalyst might be on the lookout and which might serve as relevant evidence in assessing the status of some particular psychoanalytic hypothesis. Instead, I use the technical conceptual apparatus belonging to the philosophy of science, to the extent I am familiar with it, in order to respond to challenges from that quarter. I express my appreciation of the cogency of this conceptual apparatus by responding to questions from the philosophy of science about psychoanalysis, and to the answers given to such questions, in its own terms, in a language used and easily understood, if not by most psychoanalysts, by philosophers of science themselves. For it is not the substance of psychoanalytic theory, the truth of one or another psychoanalytic hypothesis, that is at issue here. What is at issue is whether there is a methodology that is *logically* capable of assessing the scientific credibility of psychoanalytic hypotheses, and especially whether it is in principle *logically* possible (not merely practically feasible) to use data obtained in the psychoanalytic situation to test these hypotheses.

Here, then, I address a broad intellectual community, which I conceive to have a vital interest in psychoanalysis as a body of knowledge and the members of which inquire, "What is the nature of this knowledge?" That community consists not only of psychoanalysts but, among others, of social and behavioral scientists; natural scientists; and humanists; of those psychologists especially who struggle to live both with their commitment to scientific method (and, indeed, often to an experimental method) and their interest in (and in some cases practice of) psychoanalysis or any psychological treatment that is informed by a psychodynamic understanding of persons; of college students, medical students, and residents in psychiatry trying to figure out what psychoanalysis and psychoanalysts are or even to decide whether it is worthwhile to learn about the one or in some cases to try to become the other.

This book should be regarded as a logical argument about the status of psychoanalysis as a scientific discipline. As such, it needs a careful line-by-line reading, with attention directed not to some detailed account of the clinical phenomena so important to the practicing psychoanalyst, but rather primarily to an evaluation of the validity and cogency of each step in the argument.

I have avoided the use of clinical vignettes. These are likely to disturb concentration on the argument itself, and in any event to be misleading, even when illustrative, for they derive their import from a context which necessarily remains unspecified. Psychoanalytic work is a response to nuances, to an infinite variety of individual expressions of our general and abstract concepts; the more detailed and focused on the particular such a vignette is, the more likely it is to be convincing—and the more awkward become problems of confidentiality.

Those clinical examples that are present—and there are some (Breuer's case of Anna O., Freud's case of the Rat Man, Kohut's case of Mr. Z, and Luborsky's case of Miss X)—will not distract attention from the argument to the merits of clinical work or the meanings of clinical phenomena, because these examples are not offered as evidence for any hypothesis but are instead a part of the argument itself. I do allude to, and make use of, my knowledge as a clinician of the complexities of the psychoanalytic situation, but only insofar as I judge such allusions to be necessary to the argument I am making.

Justifiably or not, given the particular combination of my experience as a clinical psychoanalyst, and a background in research methodology and philosophy of science which goes back at least as far as my days both as a graduate student and medical student at the University of Chicago, I feel it is especially incumbent upon me to respond for psychoanalysis to the challenge of that emphatic negative answer to the two questions in this introduction's first paragraph. In this book, therefore, accepting this most serious responsibility (while also perhaps enjoying a fantasy of myself as a David defending his people against a Goliath), I shall propose some answers to questions about the current scientific status of psychoanalysis, indicating at the same time what I conceive to be especially difficult problems and especially promising directions for the future.

PART 1

# The Challenge

Three times, at least, the status of psychoanalysis as science has been called into question. The first two challenges may now seem to some in retrospect to have been hardly worth the bother of a response, but I cannot think that will ever be said about the third.

First, logical positivism charged that psychoanalysis was infested with theoretical terms so vague, so unconnected to empirical procedures, its hypotheses could not be empirically verified or confirmed (Nagel, 1959). But, for reasons I shall mention in Chapter 1, the philosophers of science themselves eventually rejected the logical positivists' overformal prescriptive conception of scientific theory (Suppe, 1977).

Furthermore, the pursuit by some logical positivists of a way to measure the degree of support a hypothesis receives from empirical evidence led eventually to a vacuous "enumerative inductivism." Enumerative inductivism is a name for the view that any observation entailed by a hypothesis "supports" it, and that the greater the number of such positive instances of a hypothesis the greater the degree of empirical "support." So, for example, any observation of a person who both has an unconscious conflict involving homosexual impulses and is paranoid would be held to support a hypothesis asserting there is a causal relationship between the two. The greater the number of such persons observed, the greater the degree to which the hypothesis is supported by observations.

Enumerative inductivism is vacuous, because hypotheses are under-determined by data. That is, the same data can be explained by an infinite number of hypotheses, and therefore can be held to "support" any number of quite different hypotheses. Moreover, in the example given, it may turn out that observations have been confined to paranoid persons, who perhaps do turn out, in a high percentage of cases, to have an unconscious conflict involving homosexual impulses. If nonparanoid persons are also examined, however, and these turn out in an equally high percentage of cases to have a similar conflict, or persons having an unconscious conflict involving homosexual impulses are observed and in an equal proportion of cases some turn out to be paranoid and some nonparanoid, then clearly observations of persons who both are paranoid and have such a conflict cannot in themselves be regarded to confer upon the causal hypothesis any scientific credibility at all.

In reflecting upon the inadequacy of enumerative inductivism, consider the turkey which, in predicting its own future, gives equal weight to every instance of being fed. This deluded fowl thus collects or enumerates positive instances of the universal generalization, "No matter what the day, if a turkey waits, in a specified place at a specified time, it will be fed." The sheer bulk of these positive instances supposedly provides, as they accrue, increasingly impressive and higher and higher degrees of support for the generalization. Then comes Thanksgiving. Hitchcock made his own criticism of enumerative inductivism (Leach, 1979, p. 2). He is reported to have replied to a question about what he made of the fact that someone committed murder after viewing *Psycho*, "And how many people have committed murder after viewing *The Sound of Music*?" Such considerations constitute the inadequacy of this view of the relation between hypothesis and evidence.

No scientist really accepts such a view of the relation between hypothesis and evidence. However, psychoanalysis, like other theories, as many have pointed out, has no difficulty obtaining numerous positive instances of its hypotheses, and perhaps there are those among psychoanalysts, who are not necessarily trained as scientists, who have been lulled into a false sense of security by the link between the respectable logical positivism and enumerative inductivism. Certainly some psychoanalysts have felt and still feel free to indulge in the delusion that their heaps of clinical observations, case reports, vignettes, and anecdotes do meet scientific requirements for empirical evidence.

However, Rapaport (1959b, p. 111) warned psychoanalysts that while "the evidence [for psychoanalytic hypotheses] . . . seems massive and imposing, the lack of clarification as to what constitutes a valid clinical [that is, nonexperimental] research method leaves undetermined the positive evidential weight of the confirming clinical material." He cautioned his colleagues that, because the required "canon of clinical investigation is lacking, much of the evidence for the theory remains phenomenological and anecdotal, even if its obviousness and bulk tend to lend it a semblance of objective validity."

Rapaport realized, and I agree, that formulating a canon of single subject research is critical for any approach to this problem by psychoanalysts; it is, he wrote twenty-two years ago, "urgent to reinvestigate Freud's case studies with the aim of clarifying whether or not they can yield a canon of clinical research at the present stage of our knowledge." I shall have something more to say about that in the following pages, and also in my forthcoming work *Single Subject Research*. Glymour (1974, 1980), in particular, whose analysis of the Rat Man case I shall be considering in some detail later in these pages, has made a start on the task Rapaport urges upon psychoanalysis.

In any event, as we shall see in Chapter 1, it is logical positivism itself, at least in its most distinctive form, which has fallen into disrepute. Whether or not psychoanalysis satisfies its criteria for what is science is now moot.

Second, Popper (1963, pp. 33–39) charged that psychoanalysis was incapable of meeting his criterion for demarcating science from nonscience, for its hypotheses could not be falsified by any empirical evidence. (I shall consider the criterion of falsifiability in Chapter 2.) Nothing in Popper's writing, whatever its other considerable virtues, indicated that he was informed about psychoanalysis. Those who responded to this charge had little difficulty showing that psychoanalytic hypotheses are not in principle nonfalsifiable and that some hypotheses have actually been falsified by Freud himself (Glymour, 1974, 1980; Grünbaum, 1977a, 1977b, 1978, 1979; Hospers, 1959; Salmon, 1959).

It should be said that in his animadversions Popper may have had something in mind other than the intrinsic falsifiability of psychoanalytic hypotheses. Certainly, psychoanalysts do not habitually specify in their writings just exactly what particular observations, obtained under what conditions, would be generally accepted as grounds for decisively rejecting a psychoanalytic hypothesis like the one, for example, asserting a causal relation between paranoia and an unconscious conflict involving homosexual impulses. Perhaps Popper was overimpressed by what look like attempts by some psychoanalysts to render one or another set of privileged psychoanalytic hypotheses immune from falsification (usually in the interest of protecting practice from vulgarization or erosion), or to substitute citation of authority (for example, Freud) for rigorous empirical tests as grounds for conferring credibility upon one or another hypothesis. Such attempts might lead one to question the qualifications of such psychoanalysts as scientists, but are irrelevant with respect to the question of whether psychoanalytic hypotheses are in principle nonfalsifiable.

Third, and most recently, Grünbaum (1980, 1981, 1982a, 1982b) charges that psychoanalytic hypotheses, while falsifiable, have not been shown to be scientifically credible, and, further, that it is impossible to obtain probative data in the psychoanalytic situation. Probative data are data capable of conferring such credibility upon a hypothesis by providing grounds for accepting it provisionally as true over a rival or alternative hypothesis.

Grünbaum believes that, even if it were possible to demonstrate that the values of two variables co-vary in the psychoanalytic situation, there is no way to justify evidentially the supposition that one acts as cause and the other is its effect. For the possibility of such a justification, in his view, depends upon the ability to manipulate experimentally treatments, conditions, or levels (that is, amounts) of a treatment in order to produce, measure, and above all compare the effects of different treatments, conditions, or levels, and to control or eliminate extraneous influences which might otherwise be held to be responsible for bringing about in a particular study observed differences in effects, or for preventing in a particular study such differences from manifesting themselves when they really exist. The data yielded by the nonexperimental method of free association, in contrast, are so unavoidably contaminated by extraneous influences that they are not capable of eliminating plausible alternative explanations for some set of observations "explained" by and therefore adduced as "support" for a psychoanalytic hypothesis.

Grünbaum's judgments are based on the criteria of eliminative inductivism. Eliminative inductivism is a name for the view that evidence shall count as support for a hypothesis, shall confer scientific credibility upon a hypothesis, only if:

*a*) the evidence is entailed by, is deducible from, or is a positive instance of, the hypothesis (that the evidence confirms the hypothesis is necessary, but not sufficient, for it to count as support for the hypothesis);

*b*) the evidence justifies preferring the hypothesis to some other rival hypothesis (that is, justifies believing the hypothesis rather than this rival);

*c*) the evidence has been obtained in a way that eliminates from consideration plausible alternative explanations, which otherwise might have been held to account for it.[1]

Eliminative inductivism is not newfangled; it goes back at least as far as the canons of scientific method formulated by John Stuart Mill—and probably, according to Grünbaum, further back than that. It reflects scientific practice.[2] It embodies a distinctive form of logically sophisticated reasoning, which is well-suited to the objectives of a scientist who wishes to know what statements he is justified in accepting provisionally as true of the domain he studies—"true of" in the sense of corresponding to a state of affairs in the actual world (that is, corresponding to relations between and among entities in that world).

Eliminative inductivism, therefore, is not likely to end up dismissed as an arbitrary, artificial, or perfectionistic invention of a group of scholastics. Nor will it be easy—although, I shall argue in subsequent pages, it should not be impossible—to bring psychoanalytic investigations into conformity with its standards. To appreciate more fully the force of the challenge of eliminative inductivism (described in detail in Chapter 3) requires a somewhat greater acquaintance, which is the intent of what follows in Chapters 1 and 2, with both the challenge of logical positivism and the challenge of falsificationism.

1. I shall give a more detailed precise explication of eliminative inductivism in Chapter 3.

2. Among recent excellent monographs or texts on research method and design, written from the point of view of eliminative inductivism, see especially Cook and Campbell (1979), who emphasize how to make do with quasi-experimental and nonexperimental designs in naturalistic settings; and Kazdin (1980a), who emphasizes the use of experimental designs in studies of psychotherapy.

# 1     Can Psychoanalytic Hypotheses Be Empirically Confirmed?

In this chapter, I shall describe logical positivism and the correspondence theory of truth, show to what difficulties logical positivism has fallen prey, discuss an alternative view of scientific theory, and present the way in which logical positivism challenged psychoanalysis and how that challenge was met.

## 1. Logical Positivism

Logical positivism distinguishes between synthetic and analytic statements. The first kind of statement is held to be cognitively meaningful if and only if it has empirical consequences. Such a statement is true because it, or at least one statement which logically follows from it, corresponds to some fact or set of facts in the actual world. The second kind of statement, for example, a statement of mathematics or logic, is cognitively meaningful by virtue of the rules of a language which generates it. No other statement has cognitive meaning. Logical positivism is committed to using a rigorous, precise, and unambiguous logical or formal language in order to analyze, criticize, or reconstruct the procedures and products of science.

## 2. Logical Positivism and the Correspondence Theory of Truth

Logical positivism is closely tied to some version of a correspondence theory of truth, rather than to a view of truth as relative to, or a function of, subjective states of knowledge or belief.[1] Whether or not a synthetic (that is, empirical) statement is true is determined by its correspondence with the actual world. If "s" is a sentence, then "s" is true if and only if a state of affairs s (designated by the sentence "s") obtains in the actual world. The sentence "it is snowing" is true if and only if it is snowing.[2] This formulation is apparently rather simple (deceptively so), but also, as it turns out, powerful. It does not provide us with a

1. Compare Quine (1970) and White (1970).
2. The formulation is Tarski's (1944).

general definition of truth, but it does provide us with a condition that must be met by each particular sentence capable of being empirically true or false before the predicate "true" may be applied to it.

Every statement in the language of science is either true or false. It is true if it is in accord with the actual world, and false if it is not true. That every such statement has one or the other of these two truth-values is not affected by whether or not we know its truth-value, whether or not we have a procedure to determine its truth-value, and whether or not we can prove that it is true or false.[3] A statement that is neither true nor false is not admissible to the corpus of scientific knowledge.

This is not to say that there are not problems in deciding whether to accept a statement as true or false, as corresponding (or not) to a fact or facts in the actual world. The intractability of such problems, as we shall see, has been fateful for logical positivism. However, the notion of one of its offshoots, "operationism," that meaning in science is equivalent to the operations or procedures by which the truth of a statement is empirically established or "verified," is not tenable. It is simply not the case that the application of "true" (that is, provisionally accepted as true) is permitted in science only when a statement can be logically proven to be true or there is an available procedure for direct empirical "verification" of it.

The truth or falsity of a statement does not depend on what we know but on the relation of the statement to the actual world. This relation does not change, whatever our difficulties in determining what that relation is. It has come to be generally accepted that statements in science can only be accepted provisionally as true, because with the help of new methods and in the light of new knowledge scientists revise statements previously accepted as true. Contrary to a widespread misconception of science, scientific knowledge is not a body of statements the scientist believes with absolute certainty; rather he accepts some statements provisionally as true, given evidence so far available to him. As Chomsky (1957) has pointed out in another context, scientists have criteria for deciding what is, according to the evidence, the "better" of two hypotheses, but not for deciding what is the "best" hypothesis. Here, however, it is the progressively changing state of our knowledge, and not the truth-values of statements, which is at issue.

Tarski has pointed out that semantic concepts such as "true" are used

---

3. Tarski (1969) shows that not all true statements (here he refers to analytic statements) can be proven to be true.

"in psychology, sociology, and in practically all the humanities" to describe entities in their domain, but have no application to entities in the domain of natural sciences such as physics and biology.

> Thus, a psychologist defines the so-called intelligence quotient in terms of the numbers of *true* (right) and *false* (wrong) answers given by a person to certain questions; for a historian of culture the range of objects for which a human race in successive stages of its development possesses adequate *designations* may be a topic of great significance; a student of literature may be strongly interested in the problem whether a given author always uses two given words with the same *meaning*. [1944, p. 37]

A semantic science is one that includes such entities as sentences and other linguistic expressions in the domain it studies, and that uses such semantic predicates as "true" to describe entities in its domain. I would say that psychoanalysis, which uses predicates such as ". . . makes (or does not make) sense" to describe psychological entities or events, is a semantic science. That it is accounts for the tendency to consider it a humanistic discipline. (Psychology, sociology, and linguistics have also suffered from this misconception.) This misconception may underlie the position that psychoanalysis is not a science but a hermeneutics. However, an intellectual enterprise does not fail to be scientific because of the entities it studies or the predicates it uses to describe these entities and their relations. What is distinctive about science is method not content.

## 3. The Foundering of Logical Positivism

According to a logical positivist such as Nagel, theoretical terms in psychoanalytic theory are not "*tied down to fairly definite and unambiguously specified* observable materials, by way of rules of procedure variously called 'correspondence rules,' 'coordinating definitions,' and 'operational definitions'" and "the theory is stated in language so vague and metaphorical that almost anything appears to be compatible with it" (1959, pp. 40–41). How does this critique hold up?

Logical positivism, in a version which is widely known,[4] holds that:

---

4. It is difficult to make a position so dependent on logical formalism vivid in this short space. The reader who is not familiar with the details is not likely to be enlightened by the following account. Such a reader, if interested, may eventually consult Brown (1977) and Suppe (1977), meanwhile skipping to section 4, titled "An Alternative: The Nonstatement View of Theory," on page 12.

1. A scientific theory is a set of statements, which entail other (empirical) statements as consequences.

2. The vocabulary of a scientific theory can be divided into theoretical terms, which do not correspond to anything that can be directly observed, and empirical or observation terms. Theoretical terms are linked to observation terms by coordinating definitions.

3. Statements have cognitive meaning if they are verified. Terms have cognitive meaning if they are defined by empirical operations. Such criteria of cognitive meaning are satisfied only by:

*a*) terms referring to empirical procedures of observation and measurement;

*b*) statements using just these terms or these and logical terms;

*c*) statements which, with the aid of coordinating definitions and rules of inference, entail the preceding statements.

In this view, theoretical terms are conveniences, which are logically eliminable. All statements of science are reducible or translatable into statements belonging to a neutral, theory-free, basic observation language. A scientist can confirm such statements by checking empirically to see whether they are compatible or incompatible with observations (correspond to the world as it is). Do these statements, in other words, correspond to facts? A theory is confirmable, when there are procedures for determining whether statements using no logical terms and corresponding to simple or singular facts are compatible or incompatible with its generalizations. Such a statement is compatible with a generalization when it is deducible, and therefore the phenomenon it describes is predictable, from the generalization, or when it "supports" the generalization by providing an instance of it, thus increasing its degree of "probability." [5]

Logical positivism ran into difficulties because of the overrestrictive nature of its solution to the problem of determining whether or not a statement corresponds to a fact or facts in the actual world. This is, however, as we shall see, not necessarily a reason to follow those (for example, Spence, 1982) who, seeing psychoanalysis as a species of hermeneutics rather than a science, propose rejecting the correspondence theory of truth altogether. Here, I am in accord with the naive realism of Freud (for example, 1900, p. 610), who regarded himself insofar as he

---

5. The requirement that theories be "verifiable," in the sense of "can be conclusively demonstrated or proven by evidence to be true," is no longer part of any serious proposal in the philosophy of science.

was a scientist as attempting to approximate in his statements an un-known but actual reality. The very objectives of science themselves seem to me to imply some version of a correspondence theory of truth.

The notion of a scientific theory as a set of statements has foundered on the practical difficulty of stating exhaustively the statements (includ-ing coordinating definitions) comprising any actual scientific theory, or of formulating in a formal language a set of axioms for any such theory.

The division of the vocabulary of a theory into observation terms and eliminable theoretical terms has foundered on:

1. the demonstrable usefulness to science of its theoretical terms and their apparent irreplaceability, given an adequate conception of the ex-planatory aims of science (for example, that a scientific theory makes assertions about infinite domains, therefore necessarily about unob-served entities, and about events which have not yet occurred, and therefore not observed);

2. the relative paucity in scientific work of coordinating definitions linking theoretical terms to observation terms; and

3. the failure to identify an observation language which is actually neutral and theory-free.

Theoretic terms have come to be distinguished instead from non-theoretic terms. This distinction is relativized to a particular theory. A particular theory's nontheoretic terms, while not theory-free, are inde-pendent of that theory (that is, do not require knowledge of that theory to be understood or used). A rationale for the procedures used to decide what numbers to assign to nontheoretic terms (that is, in measurement) depends upon the propositions of another presupposed theory. A term that is a nontheoretic term in one theory (in biology, for example) may be a theoretic term in a second theory (in physics, for example) pre-supposed by the first. There is no shared, theory-free, neutral, pure, "sense-data" language of empirical observation.

The adoption of empirical operations as a criterion for cognitive meaning has foundered on:

1. the fact that many procedures are used to measure the same the-oretical concept (on this criterion, each operation or procedure for mea-suring length, for example, defines a distinct concept);

2. the fact that procedures for observation, including perception, are not neutral or theory-free but depend on existing knowledge;

3. the fact that a way of measuring the degree of probability accorded a hypothesis or theory by true observation statements compatible with it (that is, a way of measuring the degree of confirmation these statements

confer upon a hypothesis or theory) continues to be elusive. (In fact, hypotheses are rather valued to the extent that they are improbable, where "improbable" refers to the extent the outcomes predicted from them are improbable.)[6]

## 4. An Alternative: The Nonstatement View of Theory

A new conception of theory in the philosophy of science (the non-statement view), to be discussed in greater detail in Part Two of this book, now challenges that of logical positivism (Giere, 1979b; Steg-müller, 1976; Suppes, 1967). This view holds that a theory is not a set of statements. Rather, theoretical work in science involves the definition of a *theoretical predicate*, such as ". . . is a classical system of particle mechanics." Such a theoretical predicate is true of a domain (for example, a set of physical things) just in case the domain satisfies certain conditions. The definition of a theoretical predicate gives the conditions a domain must satisfy for a theoretical predicate to be true of it.[7]

A theoretical predicate, while a linguistic entity, is not a statement (it is rather like other predicates, such as ". . . is red"). The definition of a theoretical predicate (in terms of the conditions which must be satisfied by a domain for the predicate to be true of it) is not an empirical statement. (No definition is.) The conditions themselves are not linguistic entities at all but states of affairs in the world, as in Tarski's (1944) definition of the predicate ". . . is true": The sentence "It is snowing" is true if and only if it is snowing (a state of affairs in the world).

In this nonstatement view of theory, the only statements that are empirically testable are *theoretical hypotheses*, which claim of a specified domain that a theoretical predicate is true of it. Only a theoretical hypothesis about a specified domain can be empirically true or false. That a theoretical predicate turns out not to be true of a particular domain (that is, some theoretical hypothesis is falsified with respect to a particular domain) does not imply the theoretical predicate is not or cannot be true of other domains. Scientists (including psychoanalysts) do not abandon useful concepts simply because they are not applicable to or satisfied by every domain.

A theoretical predicate designates a concept of a domain, a concept

6. For a fine work on confirmation and the tradition of ideas associated with it, see Carnap (1936a, 1936b). See also Brown (1977) and Suppe (1977) for discussion of these ideas and of the difficulties associated with them.

7. See technical note 1. Technical notes may be omitted without loss of continuity.

the scientist has "invented" or "discovered," a way of looking at the world, an insight (however partial) into its structure or nature. Since a theoretical predicate is not an entity that can be true or false—it is not a statement—and the definition of a theoretical predicate is a decision about the usage of a term and not a statement that can be empirically true or false, talk of confirmation or falsification of a theory, or of the confirmability or falsifiability of a theory in the usual sense, on this view is incoherent.

## 5. Psychoanalysis and the Challenge of Logical Positivism

Even if a theory were to be regarded as a set of statements, Nagel's examples of so-called propositions of psychoanalytic theory do not in fact represent a correct analysis of that theory. A critique of psychoanalytic theory can indeed only be evaluated, if we know what version or statement of that theory is the object of criticism. Not even Freud has provided one specific, determinate formulation, which is then the candidate for tests and revisions. Choosing to confine oneself to Freud's corpus, as many philosophers of science do, is no solution. Even here, one can ask, "To which theory of Freud's do you refer?"

It is, of course, the responsibility of psychoanalysis to provide a standard formulation for others to examine. However, focusing on possible "methodological" defects in the formulation of psychoanalytic theory is premature in the absence of agreement about what the nontheoretic concepts, the theoretic concepts, and the domains of psychoanalysis are, and what the substantive testable theoretical claims about these different domains made by psychoanalysis are. I shall take up this problem in Part Two of this book.

Nagel's criticism, mentioned in the previous section, that the theoretical terms of psychoanalysis are so vague or have so little empirical content that its propositions cannot be confirmed receives a more or less adequate response (although different kinds of response) from Salmon (1959), Pap (1959), Danto (1959), and Hospers (1959).

Salmon's position is representative. Suppose the principle of psychic determinism is that events such as parapraxes, dreams, and neurotic symptoms have as their causes such psychic events as conscious or unconscious wishes, and that the relation between these causes and the phenomena of interest may be expressed by either deterministic or probabilistic laws. This principle "is an empirical postulate subject to confirmation or disconfirmation by empirical evidence; it asserts the existence of definite relations among events; but the relation may be either deterministic or probabilistic; and it specifies that the 'causes' involved are of a rather specific sort" (Salmon, 1959, pp. 256–257).

> . . . it is necessary that there be independent evidence for the existence of [a] psychic mechanism, apart from the specific item it is supposed to explain. Other parts of psychoanalytic theory indicate what the independent evidence is. The theory gives a limited list of inferred entities such as unconscious feelings, desires, impulses, conflicts, and defense mechanisms. In some cases, at least, the theory states that such entities are created (with a high degree of probability) under certain specifiable conditions. The occurrence of such conditions constitutes independent inductive evidence for the existence of the entity. Furthermore, according to the theory, if one of these unconscious psychic entities exists, it is possible under specifiable conditions to elicit a certain kind of conscious entity (which may go under the same name without the qualification "unconscious"). Free association, hypnosis, and narcosynthesis are ways of eliciting the unconscious entity. It is not that the subject becomes aware of an unconscious entity—there is a sense in which this is impossible by definition. Rather, according to the theory, the occurrence of the conscious entity (or the report of it if one insists upon excluding introspective evidence) under the specified conditions constitutes inductive evidence for the existence of the inferred entity at an earlier time. Other items of behavior such as slips, dreams, and neurotic symptoms constitute further inductive evidence for the existence of the inferred entity. It may be, and often is, the case that none of these items of evidence is by itself very conclusive, but we must keep in mind that inductive inference often involves a concatenation of evidence each item of which is quite inconclusive. Nevertheless, the whole body of such evidence may well be conclusive.[8] [Salmon, 1959, pp. 258–259]

Others argue in response to criticisms such as Nagel's that:

1. "theoretical" concepts in psychoanalysis are disposition concepts, and therefore actually pretheoretic not theoretic concepts, but these concepts are heuristic, because they mark a need for explanation (Pap, 1959);

2. the explanatory and predictive accuracy of a theory is independent of the ontology to which it subscribes, so that psychoanalytic theory cannot be dismissed because of disbelief in the existence of entities its theoretical terms appear to denote (Danto, 1959);

8. This last point bears resemblance to a position taken by Glymour (1980).

3. even though any one of a number of alternatives constitutes a necessary condition for a particular inferred event or state, the list is finite, so that confirming instances of a psychoanalytic hypothesis are identifiable (Hospers, 1959).

Eventually, logical positivism took the position that:

1. only some of a theory's theoretical terms must be linked to observation terms by coordinating definitions;

2. a theory (a set of statements) as a whole, and not necessarily each statement in the theory, must have empirical consequences, and is in fact tested as a whole with each empirical test of one of its statements.

On this version, psychoanalytic theory is "confirmable." Instances of its propositions are not difficult to find. Such observations are compatible with, apparently confirm, and, if one is an enumerative inductivist, can be held (mistakenly, as we have noted) to "support" to some degree, statements belonging to psychoanalytic theory.

I shall drive this last point home again with another example, since some clinicians seem especially prone to accept the idea that a clinical observation which satisfies both the antecedent and the consequent of a universal generalization (such an observation is called an instance of such a hypothesis) goes toward justifying provisional acceptance of that hypothesis, and that the greater the number of such "confirming" instances, the more that provisional acceptance of the hypothesis is justified. The clinician then responds enthusiastically to each confirming instance, and assumes that piling up these confirming instances will suffice to convince.

Suppose the hypothesis is: For all individuals in a domain of humans, if an individual suffers from a neurosis (antecedent), then that individual has a sexual disorder (consequent). (All neurotics have sexual disorders.) An instance of this hypothesis is a specified member of this domain who suffers from a neurosis (and therefore satisfies the antecedent) and who also has a sexual disorder (and therefore satisfies the consequent).

There are three difficulties with this clinician's beliefs about the relation between hypothesis and evidence. One, the terms "neurosis" and "sexual disorder" may be used, phenomena may be interpreted, or cases may be selected in such a way that confirming instances are easy to obtain. Two, and more important, no number of observations of neurotic individuals who also have sexual disorders can rule out as impossible the existence somewhere of a decisive counterexample: the individual who is neurotic but has no sexual disorder. Such a counterexample is a decisive refutation, if the generalization is held to hold universally. That is, even one such counterexample suffices to make the universal generalization false—no matter how many confirming instances have been observed. Three, and most important, there are usually other plausible hypotheses which also entail the confirming observation statement and in that sense "explain" the confirming instance.

Of course, in a reductio ad absurdum of logical positivism, one may say that there is a circumstance in which instances of a hypothesis conclusively "confirm" it. If a domain is finite and it is feasible to observe every individual with respect to satisfying both antecedent and consequent, and all terms in the hypothesis are nontheoretic, then a hypothesis is an empirical generalization. Logically, it is equivalent to the conjunction of all confirming observation statements. One might conceive that such a generalization could be decisively "confirmed" by these observation statements. However, this is not usually what is meant by "confirmation." One does not give a reason or justification for belief, when it is impossible not to believe—when the relation between generalization and a set of observation statements is logical equivalence.[9]

9. For discussions of problems in the logic of confirmation, including the so-called paradoxes of confirmation, see Hempel (1965) and Scheffler (1963).

# 2     Can Psychoanalytic Hypotheses Be Falsified?

In this chapter, I shall present Popper's view of science; the criterion of falsifiability he uses to demarcate scientific from non-scientific statements; the way in which he deals with the call for theory-free data; his use of the differentiation between the context of discovery and the context of justification; what he means by "testing a hypothesis rigorously"; Platt's systematic application of this view of science; problems with this view of science; and the way in which this view of science challenged psychoanalysis and how that challenge was met.

## 1. Science

An image of the scientist's activities, quite different in some ways from that of the logical positivists, arises from Popper's response (1959a) to the difficulties encountered when emphasis in characterizing the scientist's activities is on confirming hypotheses.

The scientist wants to make true statements about the world. The world is the world of brute fact, out there, independent of his interests, acts, and cognitive limits. The world guards its secrets.

The scientist makes what Popper calls "bold conjectures" about the world. The scientist has a method for subjecting such conjectures to rigorous tests. He does not at any time claim to have discovered the only, the final, the certain truth about the world. He does not at any time claim to possess the best guess he or anyone else will ever make about the world. He does claim at a particular time only that his conjecture so far stands up better to rigorous empirical tests than do rival conjectures. He accepts that, in later competitions with other alternatives, this same conjecture may fail such tests and require revision or rejection.

In science, no conjecture about the world is confirmed in vacuo (for example, through a piling up of positive instances consistent with it). No conjecture about the world is in and of itself confirmed by evidence. It is always evaluated relative to some rival. The degree of its acceptance is simply the extent to which at any particular time it is considered better than its comparable rivals.

Scientific hypotheses exclude possibilities, and to one degree or another select from the set of possible worlds those possible worlds which, following such exclusion, remain candidates for the actual world. The more possibilities a hypothesis excludes, the more informative it is. The more we know about what cannot be true of the actual world among all the things that might be true of it, the more we know about it.

For a hypothesis to be considered scientific, then, it must be capable of selecting, among what are merely possible characteristics of a domain, those that are actual characteristics of the domain. It must state minimally that of all the things that might be true of a domain, there is at least one that is not true. A hypothesis must as part of its content exclude at least one characterization of a domain. The more possible characterizations it excludes, the more informative it is, and the greater its content is considered to be.

The work of the scientist, like that of the psychoanalyst as therapist, is mostly a clearing-away-the-underbrush kind of work. The psychoanalyst draws attention to and tries to understand the analysand's defenses, especially those which are obstacles to the analysand's saying what he is already aware he wants, thinks, and feels. The psychoanalyst expects, then, that given the characteristics of the psychoanalytic situation, what the analysand unknowingly wants, thinks, and feels can and will gradually emerge and be uttered.[1] In this sense, the psychoanalyst does not impose a hypothesis about what is true of the analysand upon the utterances of the analysand. Rather, he chips away at interferences, he notices aloud the analysand's observed reluctances to speak, so that, following a clarification of the analysand's reasons for such reluctances, the analysand can tell the psychoanalyst with increasing clarity and explicitness what is on his mind.[2]

The scientist, on the other hand, strives to clear away impediments to knowledge of the world (for example, statements about the world that are plausible but false) by arguing from empirical evidence what cannot be true of the world. The scientist, like the psychoanalyst in his therapeutic work, believes that what is true is strong; he expects it will emerge unscathed from, it is what will survive out of, his research activities.

The scientist's desire for the truth about the world is unquenchable.

1. Stone (1961) characterizes the dilemmas the psychoanalyst traverses in creating and maintaining the psychoanalytic situation.
2. S. Ritvo has drawn my attention to a presentation of this view of the psychoanalyst's interventions by Searl (1936).

He wants to know that unknown reality lying beyond the boundaries of his sense, beyond his phenomenal experience tinted and shaded as it is by preconception and presupposition. His statements, either true or false, are timelessly so, but he does not ever know certainly which are true. He does know which statements he is more willing to accept than others. The statements he accepts he accepts provisionally. His knowledge of reality is always approximate. The more statements about reality he is able to discard as false, the more distinct his image of reality becomes. As Freud (1900, p. 610) put it, the scientist replaces one "conceptual scaffolding" for another if that will bring him nearer to something "that approximates more closely to the unknown reality."

## 2. Theory and Data

There are no theory-free sense-data serving as the irreducible arbiters of what is true and what is false. The following passage from Freud, important in connection with this point, is also relevant in considering other problems connected with the relation between theory and data.

> Even at the stage of description it is not possible to avoid applying certain abstract ideas to the material in hand, ideas derived from somewhere or other but certainly not from the new observations alone. Such ideas—which will later become the basic concepts of the science—are still more indispensable as the material is further worked over. They must at first necessarily possess some degree of indefiniteness; there can be no question of any clear delimitation of their content. So long as they remain in this condition, we come to an understanding about their meaning by making repeated references to the material of observations from which they appear to have been derived, but upon which, in fact, they have been imposed. Thus, strictly speaking, they are in the nature of conventions—although everything depends on their not being arbitrarily chosen but determined by their having significant relations to the empirical material, relations that we seem to sense before we can clearly recognize and demonstrate them. [1915, p. 117]

What the scientist perceives is in part determined by what is out there and in part by his knowledge and theories. Many factors constrain what he is able to observe. These include that his knowledge is inevitably deficient; his procedures for making observations are inadequate; and one or another presuppositions upon which his use of these procedures is based may be false. The content and formulation of the simplest observation statements are determined and constrained by conceptual decisions about what individual entities and what properties of or relations among these entities are to be included in (or excluded from) the domain the scientist chooses to study.

The scientist maintains in patience a certain amount of stubborn faith that what he thinks is so may in fact be so despite inevitably imperfect observations. At the same time, insofar as he believes not only that the world is a symbolic creation but that it is as it is independent of his knowledge of it (Edelson, 1976), he is also committed to accept that, however attached he is to his hypotheses, these must still be held provisionally. If they are false, sooner or later, and certainly in the long run, intransigent brute facts will insist themselves upon theory-soaked but also reality-fitted senses. To the extent he has confidence in his hypotheses about the nature of that unknown reality whose properties, he conjectures, account for his experience, he will obtain data in a way that challenges these hypotheses by putting them in competition with other hypotheses. He makes these challenges as difficult as possible to evade, because surviving such challenges makes his hypotheses strong.

## 3. The Context of Discovery and the Context of Justification

An enumeration of observation statements about individual entities never logically entails a universal generalization. Hypotheses, as we have seen, are underdetermined by data. That is, the truth of the same set of observation statements is consistent with the truth of many different generalizations.

The only logically warranted generalization from a set of observation statements is one that is a mere conjunction of these statements. However, a scientist cannot rest content with a generalization that merely summarizes his observations. He is not content even with an extension of such a generalization, which holds beyond his particular experience. He wants to know what hypothetical entities, what relations between these, what inapparent formal structures, what attributes of reality unknowable from particular experiences of it, account for such generalizations, and for as many such generalizations, in as many different empirical domains, as possible.

Sometimes the problem of induction (that is, how can we get from particulars of experience to universal generalizations about the world?) is formulated in such a way that it sounds as if the scientist requires logical warrant to squeeze a generalization or hypothesis out of the particulars of his experience. No such justification can be provided him. Ideas are not squeezed from data as stock from beef, but rather are invented to order data, are related to data as numbered hooks are to coats (the tropes are Einstein's).

Insight is a gift. There is no algorithm or explicit automatic procedure a scientist may follow that guarantees he will detect even one significant order, pattern, or relationship in empirical phenomena. Similarly, there is no infallible route to the correct explanation of an event or an order, pattern, or relationship in empirical phenomena once detected. There are no rules that guarantee a scientist will draw the correct curve through a set of data-points, out of the many curves he might draw, or that he will formulate the correct equation to generate his data, out of the many equations that will also generate his data. There is no explicit set of instructions he may follow that guarantees he will make a successful guess about which of a number of possible worlds is the actual world. There is no one who can tell the scientist with certainty how to get where he wants to go.

The scientist invents concepts and hypotheses in the context of discovery and tests hypotheses in the context of justification. In the context of discovery, the scientist runs risks—that he will pursue the wrong line, try to answer a dead-end question, make a guess that he does not know is in fact false. He may reason from repeated experiences or he may leap to conclusions from a single experience. He may use a heuristic rule of thumb, such as analogy, or he may come to a conjecture in a dream. He may struggle to solve a practical problem or play games with ideas.[3]

If man is a tabula rasa and his thought is the result of experience, one naturally wants to find a justification for his conjectures about the world in the particulars of his experience. In the absence of such a bias (typically, a bias of the logical positivists), one might well assume instead that man has a rich innate endowment, predisposing and enabling him to jump to certain kinds of conclusions about the nature of reality—even when experience is singular, fragmentary, debased, and insufficient to grant logical warrant to such conclusions.[4] Man's innate structure is such that he leaps to logically unwarranted conclusions—his curse and his blessing. The scientist is faced inevitably then with a profusion of contradictory conclusions and with a problem of evaluation.

3. Hanson (1958, especially chapter 4) has a different view of discovery in science. So does Rozeboom (1961). Both of these works deserve attention from those interested in the question "How is the scientist led to formulate his concepts and hypotheses?"

4. Chomsky (1957, 1972) discusses this assumption and its implications for a science of linguistics.

That problem is how to determine which conclusion to prefer and choose over its plausible comparable alternatives.

How does the scientist by testing hypotheses in the context of justification eliminate what cannot be true of the world? A hypothesis which claims that certain characterizations of the actual world do not obtain may be decisively falsified by discovering that any one of these characterizations does in fact obtain. Any hypothesis which makes no such claims, which excludes no possibilities, cannot be decisively falsified. The investigator who seeks positive instances to "confirm" such a hypothesis runs the risk of making and "confirming" a pseudoassertion, a tautology or definition, which provides no information about the actual world. It is incapable of falsification, just because it does not exclude any state of affairs at all (like the logical truth "it is raining or it is not raining," with which any observation is consistent). (It is not always easy to tell what statement in the theoretical writings of such a discipline as psychoanalysis, apparently about the actual world, is instead a proposal to use a term in a certain way or merely a logical truth.)

It follows that a clinical investigator should not then be trying to "confirm" a hypothesis by enumerating more and more instances (clinical observations) consistent with it. The clinical investigator whose habit of mind leads him to seek out positive instances in an effort to garner support for a hypothesis, rather than to subject it to rigorous test in competition with other hypotheses, does run the risk of committing himself to a weak hypothesis. He is more likely to produce ideology, mythology, or politically motivated position papers than science. He does not narrow the set of what can be true of the actual world.

This is not to imply that the clinical facts are somehow unimportant. Clinical facts, properly obtained, can be used to determine in the context of justification whether one hypothesis is better supported than another by evidence. Clinical facts can be used by the clinical investigator to knock rival hypotheses out of contention. Furthermore, in the context of discovery, unexpected clinical facts especially provoke clinical investigators to conjecture. If a fact is surprising because it is incompatible with a clinical investigator's conceptions or knowledge, he wants to explain it. To satisfy this urge, he formulates a hypothesis of which the surprising fact is a logical consequence.

## 4. Testing Hypotheses

Given as true (1) a hypothesis, (2) the statements of the conditions holding at the time of the test of that hypothesis, and (3) statements of the auxiliary assumptions underlying the use of particular methods for collecting or analyzing data, the scientist deduces by the rules of logic (4) a statement describing what, on the basis of these givens or premises, is the expected or predicted outcome of a research study.

The hypothesis is a universal generalization. Suppose that the result of the research study is that the predicted outcome does not occur (the statement deduced from the given premises turns out to be false). Then—since there is held to be no question about the truth of the statements of conditions and auxiliary assumptions, and there is a question about the truth of the hypothesis—according to the rules of logic, it is the hypothesis that must be false. The outcome that has actually been observed is a counterexample of the universal generalization. It refutes that generalization decisively.

Among auxiliary assumptions often assumed by the scientist to be true are the following:

*a*) Other things are equal. The scientist has adequate knowledge. He is warranted in asserting that there are no unknown facts or events, and no extraneous (unmeasured or unconsidered) factors, which could be held to account for the result of the research study.

*b*) There is no significant error. The scientist has made no systematic error in carrying out his procedures, and there is no fault in his instruments leading to systematic error, which could be held to account for the result of the research study.

*c*) There is no significant bias. The scientist has not through his own actions, either wittingly or unwittingly, subtly or obviously, influenced or interfered with the result of the research study.

*d*) There are no false theoretical presuppositions. The scientist is justified in accepting as true the theoretical presuppositions underlying the methods and operations, including instruments, he uses to collect or analyze data, as well as the assumptions he makes about the type of data collected, the way in which instruments work, and the adequacy (reliability and validity) of the data these instruments generate.

The scientist's strategy is to predict not just any outcome but an outcome that is unlikely to be true, because of other knowledge the scientist has, or because there are so many other logically possible outcomes incompatible with the one predicted that could just as well be true. It must not only be possible for the deduced outcome to be false, it must be unlikely that it is true. The more novel, unexpected, and surprising the prediction is, the less likely it is to be true, because so much of the scientist's knowledge either does not imply this predicted outcome or implies that it will not occur. Thus, the hypothesis actually runs some risk of being falsified.

The more precise the prediction is (for example, "John is 181.54 pounds"), the more logical possibilities (here, for example, a very large number of other weights) it excludes. Therefore, in competition with all these possibilities, the less likely it is to be the one that is true. It is in this sense that "improbable" hypotheses—that is, hypotheses from which improbable outcomes are deduced—are valued in science.

No procedure should be used to determine whether the deduced statement is true or false that itself depends upon or presupposes the truth of the deduced outcome. For, in that case, the truth of the deduced statement is logically guaranteed by the argument, which contains that statement as a hidden given or premise. The deduced statement will then be true irrespective of the truth or falsity of the hypothesis. Its truth cannot be surprising or unlikely.

The scientist does everything possible—this often requires considerable inventiveness—to close the loophole that the discovered falsity of the deduced statement of outcome entails the falsity of the statements of conditions or auxiliary assumptions rather than the falsity of the tested hypothesis. Upon the scientist's commitment on sound grounds to refuse to escape through one of these loopholes to evade falsification of his hypothesis depends the judgment that it is in fact just the hypothesis that has been at risk in predicting the outcome and that it is the hypothesis therefore which has been subject to rigorous test.

In general, a scientist will give preference to, or choose to test, those hypotheses with most content, scope, and precision.[5] These are the hypotheses most vulnerable to falsification, and therefore also the hypotheses which, when they have survived empirical tests, have survived the most rigorous tests, and thus have provided the strongest justification for the scientist's provisional acceptance of them as true.

If two incompatible hypotheses about the same domain are comparable in content, scope, and precision, then they are most likely to be seen by a scientist as rivals—fitting competitors—and pitted against each other in rigorous empirical tests. A good part of the work of a scientist may be to bring a hypothesis to a point (with regard to its content, scope, and precision) such that it can be regarded as a serious and appropriate alternative to some other hypothesis. Most debates in the so-

---

5. For discussion of various of these criteria, in addition to Popper (1959a, especially pp. 41, 69, and chapter 6), see Carnap (1958, pp. 15–22) and Hildebrand, Laing, and Rosenthal (1977, pp. 26–27).

cial sciences, in psychology and psychoanalysis, and in clinical research about the respective merits of hypotheses do not actually pit comparable hypotheses against one another. Given this circumstance, any conclusive decision about respective merits is unlikely.

## 5. A Systematic Application of a Falsificationist View of Scientific Method

Platt (1964) in his presentation of strong inference describes how a domain can be systematically investigated by formulating rival hypotheses in such a way that possibilities with regard to what is true of the domain are progressively eliminated. For example, the most general incompatible hypotheses about a domain are clearly stated, and one of these, by whatever means will do the trick, is falsified. Assuming that the rival hypotheses form an exhaustive set of possibilities and provisionally accepting the surviving hypothesis as true, then, if that hypothesis is true, one of a pair of less general hypotheses should be true. Again, using whatever method is available and appropriate, one of these two hypotheses is falsified. The process is repeated.

This way of proceeding resembles that employed by a clinician studying a single case who, using psychodiagnostic data and information from interviews, for example, rules out possibilities listed in a differential diagnosis. Is this a case of neurosis or psychosis? Given evidence which both favors neurosis and rules out psychosis, is it this particular neurosis or that particular neurosis?

Platt claims that, whenever rapid advance occurs in a discipline (for example, molecular biology), the use of the strategy of strong inference (avoidance of overdependence on any particular method of investigation, and emphasis instead on orderly and efficient conceptualization and on the progressive elimination of rival hypotheses) is responsible. One field of science moves forward much faster than another not because of the "tractability of the subject" (its relative lack of complexity or its susceptibility to mathematicization or quantification) but because of an intellectual factor. It is "not a matter of measurement . . . but a matter of formulating logical alternatives." Scientists in a fast-moving field "formally and explicitly and regularly" formulate rival hypotheses; devise "a crucial experiment (or several of them), with alternative possible outcomes, each of which will, as nearly as possible, exclude one or more of the hypotheses"; carry out the experiment so as to get a reliable result; and then, depending on this result, formulate a further set of rival hypotheses "to refine the possibilities that remain."

Platt believes an emphasis on disproof and on multiple hypotheses is the keystone. He quotes Bacon's "[To man] it is granted only to proceed at first by negatives, and at last to end in affirmatives after exclusion has been exhausted," and Rushton's "A theory which cannot be mortally endangered cannot be alive" (pp. 349–350). On the formulation of multiple hypotheses as a means of preventing dogmatic adherence to a belief, he quotes Chamberlin:

> The moment one has offered an original explanation for a phe-nomenon which seems satisfactory, that moment affection for his intellectual child springs into existence, and as the explanation grows into a definite theory his parental affections cluster about his offspring and it grows more and more dear to him. . . . There springs up also unwittingly a pressing of the theory to make it fit the facts and a pressing of the facts to make them fit the theory. . . .
>
> To avoid this grave danger, the method of multiple working hy-potheses is urged. It differs from the simple working hypothesis in that it distributes the effort and divides the affections. . . . Each hypothesis suggests its own criteria, its own means of proof, its own method of developing the truth, and if a group of hypotheses encompass the subject on all sides, the total outcome of means and of methods is full and rich. [P. 350]

Platt contrasts orientation to a problem and exclusion of hypotheses, the "regular and explicit use of alternative hypotheses and sharp exclu-sions," with preoccupation in less effective fields with a particular method rather than problem, and preference in these fields for un-systematically "feeling one's way" toward hypotheses. In more ef-fective fields, the scientist usually begins with a hypothesis about his subject—for example, that DNA is a long helical molecule. Suppose this hypothesis survives an effort to reject it in favor of some other; the other instead is falsified. Then, given this result, the scientist might ex-plicitly pose as testable incompatible alternatives that the helix has two or three strands, that the strands stay together or separate when the cell divides, and so on.

Platt contrasts "those who are looking to see if there is one thing that can be understood" with "those who keep saying it is very complicated and nothing can be understood." The triumphs in molecular biology are achieved by those who have chosen to use "oversimplified" model sys-tems and "have not fallen to the kind of men who justify themselves by saying, 'no two cells are alike,' regardless of how true that may ulti-mately be" (pp. 348–349).

I think it is especially important in clinical research that the complexity of a domain of study should not be used to counsel despair and inaction. Another version of such counsel starts with the assertion that, in some philosophical sense, everything is related to everything, so there is no point in isolating particular variables and studying their relation. But it is an empirical question, and not a philosophical question, whether variables are related or not, in some technical sense of the word "related." For example, variables are or are not statistically associated or correlated, do or do not have a linear correlation, are or are not related by a one-to-one function.

## 6. Problems with a Falsificationist View of Scientific Method

Despite Popper's efforts to develop a concept of "corroboration" based on his view of science, it is difficult to make explicit the logical warrant for even provisionally accepting a hypothesis on the grounds that it has not yet been falsified or that so far all rivals to it have been falsified. If a predicted outcome occurs, the scientist's confidence in his decision to accept provisionally his hypothesis will always at the least depend upon his ability to carry out the study in such a way that plausible alternative hypotheses consistent with the truth of the deduced statement of outcome have been eliminated as viable alternatives to the scientist's hypothesis in accounting for that outcome. But the scientist usually cannot know that he has explicitly stated, much less excluded, all possible alternative hypotheses.

Platt strikes a different note, because he is not thinking of alternative hypotheses all consistent with the same outcome but of incompatible hypotheses each of which entails a different one of a set of possible outcomes. "Do the bonds alternate in benzene or are they equivalent? If the first, there should be five disubstituted derivatives; if the second, three. And three it is" (Platt, 1964, p. 35). However, the adequacy of Platt's version of falsificationism seems to depend on the feasibility of constructing a theoretical characterization of a domain in such a way that a different member of a small set of mutually exclusive possibilities is entailed by each different rival hypothesis. That construction may not always be feasible; even if it is, the crucial experiment is a rare bird in many if not most sciences, including those which can make use of an experimental methodology.

There are other difficulties with the falsificationist view of science.

*a*) The falsificationist's view of theory as a set of statements is challenged by the nonstatement view of theory.

*b*) It is not the case that all hypotheses of interest to a scientist are universal generalizations. Furthermore, a probabilistic hypothesis, which excludes no possibility as impossible, cannot be conclusively falsified.

*c*) The scientist's response to discovering that a logical consequence of a hypothesis is false is by no means an automatic rejection of the hypothesis as false. No amount of methodological legislation can make the rejection of the hypothesis automatic when it is falsified by such a discovery, because scientific advance has at least once or twice depended upon some scientist's refusal to reject a hypothesis under just these circumstances. This fact calls for what I call a voluntaristic conception of scientific method.[6]

The scientist does not respond automatically but must choose how to respond to an apparent falsification of a hypothesis.

Certainly a scientist wants to stretch his hypotheses as far as they will go, to subject them severely to as rigorous tests as he can devise, in order to eliminate as many as possible, and thereby add strength to those remaining. So, ordinarily, a scientist chooses to commit himself to accept the truth of, and therefore does not test, his statements of conditions and auxiliary assumptions. He designs the test of a hypothesis so that his acceptance of these statements is justifiable. He does nothing to call forth question of them. Then, if a statement of outcome, deduced from the conjunction of the hypothesis and statements of conditions and auxiliary assumptions, turns out to be false, the scientist has chosen to commit himself to reject the hypothesis as false.

A scientist also designs a test of his hypothesis to rule out plausible alternative hypotheses which the scientist realizes might be claimed before or after the fact to account as well as his hypothesis for the outcome he predicts. The degree of success (never complete) of his efforts toward this end is relative to his choice (which depends on his insight) of a set of plausible comparable alternative hypotheses, all of which are consistent with that outcome. Since it can never be claimed that the choice of alternatives exhaust the set of possible alternative hypotheses (even the set of equally plausible, really comparable alternative hypotheses), no research design can guarantee that no other alternative to a hypothesis can ever be put forth to account for the outcome predicted

6. The word "voluntaristic" is borrowed from T. Parsons, who used it to formulate a theory of action in which the concept of choice is central, but who did not, as far as I know, apply it to scientific method.

from it. (If one should eventually be so put forth, another study must be designed to rule it out as well.) Of course, to fail to rule out obvious plausible alternatives to a hypothesis makes the test of it less than rigorous.

It does happen, this account notwithstanding, that a scientist may refuse to accept that the falsifying observation demands refutation or revision of his hypothesis. Such a refusal is not rare in science. Edelson (1954) has given an account, for example, of the way in which proponents of "the principle of the conservation of energy" refused to accept its falsification by data to the contrary in test after test over years. (Indeed, especially in the case of a hypothesis that has survived many previous tests, a refusal to accept an apparent falsification of it may be more common than the simple acceptance on the basis of a test that it must be rejected or revised.)

To support his decision to refuse to reject the hypothesis, a scientist may withdraw his prior acceptance of one or more auxiliary assumptions or his characterization of conditions at the time of his test. He may speculate that his knowledge of the situation was incomplete, that his procedures for observation were inadequate to the task they were called upon to do, or that the assumptions underlying the procedure he used were questionable. Of course, any or all of these speculations may in fact be correct, although others may wish that the scientist had seen fit not to give his assent to a characterization of conditions or auxiliary assumptions only to withdraw it when things do not go his way. Science is not a playground game.

However, in clinical research and in the social sciences generally, assertions about the dubiety of characterizations of conditions or auxiliary assumptions are indeed plausible. For these fields, the choice sometimes seems to be between giving up rigorous tests altogether and, accepting the results of tests, rejecting one proposed promising hypothesis after another. The problem for these sciences is to bring knowledge of situations, procedures, and hypotheses to the point at which hypotheses can be rigorously tested.

If the withdrawal of prior acceptance of statements about conditions or auxiliary assumptions is not to be simply a vicious ad hoc device for rescuing false hypotheses, then the rescued hypothesis must be considered on temporary probation until one or both of two tasks can be completed.

The first task is to consider revising the statement of conditions. Suppose the conditions were not what the scientist thought them to be.

Then he should make unexpected predictions about what must have been true of the situation to account together with the hypothesis for the outcome obtained. This new hypothesis about the conditions under which the previous hypothesis was tested must itself be independently tested.

Second, adequate new procedures, capable of the required degree of precision, must be developed for carrying out observations. Or alternative procedures must be used in whose underlying assumptions the scientist has confidence. These new or alternative procedures may be used with the expectation that now the original deduced observation statement will turn out to be true.

These tasks, the program a hypothesis sometimes sets for a science, may take years to achieve, if indeed they are ever achieved. It may also take years to decide they cannot be achieved, during which the hypothesis on probation may gradually be displaced by another. (Is it appropriate to characterize as a scientific "revolution," as Kuhn does, the outcome of a race between changing contenders over a long obstacle-ridden course?)

With regard to the first task, a disappointed scientist may conjecture that there must have been an additional condition, an unknown feature of the situation, to explain the unpredicted obtained outcome. Yet, such an existential generalization (for example, "there is somewhere in the situation an individual entity, such that . . .") cannot itself be decisively falsified. The scientist might look forever in an infinite universe and never find such an individual, though it may still be somewhere.

By the criterion of falsifiability, such an existential generalization is of course not a scientific hypothesis. Considering that planets, chemical elements, and events in childhood have been discovered by such postulation, this is an apparently paradoxical consequence of Popper's falsifiability criterion of demarcation. However, although the scientist may conjecture what the unknown feature of the situation must be, he cannot usually, without conjoining this conjecture to a falsifiable hypothesis, predict when, where, and how that unknown feature can be found.

The test of the hypothesis about the unknown condition often requires equipment necessary to make the predicted observation which the scientist does not yet have. It is the case that such an ad hoc "prediction" about the situation, since always possibly true, cannot be rejected absolutely. But neither, at the same time, if the viciously ad hoc is to be avoided at least in the long run, can it be used indefinitely though unfulfilled to rescue the hypothesis which otherwise would have been falsified.

However, if the scientist chooses to devote his entire life looking for the condition he predicts must be there, or waiting for the means to make an observation, in order not to reject his hypothesis, that choice cannot be forbidden him by any methodological rule. Science is a gamble. It is part of science that the scientist chooses freely to take a path which may lead either to great achievement (the discovery of something no one thought was there) or a wasted career.

Similarly, a scientist may decide to withdraw his acceptance of some auxiliary assumption about the relative absence of systematic error. He reasons, for example, that a characterization of a domain is an idealization which may be only approximately applicable to the domain. While such a characterization is therefore, strictly speaking, not true, he may decide it is the closest he can come at the time to an approximation of what is true. What degree of deviance from the predicted outcome is acceptable in continuing to regard a characterization of a domain as approximately applicable? There is more room for discretion here than is usually recognized.

A scientist may reason that the difference between the predicted and obtained outcome results from factors that are relatively unimportant in view of his hypothesis (although these same factors may very well be important in the light of another hypothesis). He may adopt a theory of error justifying his decision to regard the difference between the outcome predicted and the outcome obtained to be the consequence of numerous, random, nonsystematic, but relatively unimportant factors, rather than of some unknown systematic factor.

*d*) A final problem with the falsificationist view is that observation statements are themselves corrigible. They depend on the domain chosen, the adequacy of available measurement procedures, and intersubjective agreement, any one of which can change. To support his decision to refuse to reject a hypothesis, a scientist may withdraw his acceptance from a basic observation statement. The criterion of acceptance or rejection of an observation statement—what Popper compares to a verdict by a jury—is intersubjective agreement. "Intersubjective" implies that the observation is at least in principle repeatable. (If an observation were not repeatable, the result of any empirical test could be evaded by simply refusing to accept it; under these circumstances, it would indeed be impossible to prevent a scientist's subsequent refusal to accept an observation, should the consequences of accepting it be unpalatable.)

A verdict about an observation, like any verdict, is subject to collective error and revision. Popper points out that, contra logical positivism, basic observation statements do not, therefore, provide a foundation for logically warranted certainty in science.

> Science does not rest upon solid bedrock. The bold structure of its theories rises, as it were, above a swamp. It is like a building erected on piles. The piles are driven down from above into the swamp, but not down to any natural or 'given' base; and if we stop driving the piles deeper, it is not because we have reached firm ground. We simply stop when we are satisfied that the piles are firm enough to carry the structure, at least for the time being. [Popper, 1959a, p. 111]

The choice of a domain sets some constraints upon what can be a basic observation statement, because it fixes of what kind of individuals anything can be predicated and what sorts of properties or relations it makes sense to predicate of such individuals in that domain. Choice of a domain determines to some extent what names and predicates will be available to a scientist in formulating a basic observation statement, and therefore what kind of statements can be used to describe individuals or events.

Therefore, whether a scientist is able to make an observation, whether something is a fact for him, depends in part at least upon his knowledge of a domain and hypotheses about it, as well as his knowledge of the procedures—and the assumptions underlying these—used to make the observations. To see anything in other terms, outside these boundaries, requires a strenuous creative act, a difficult struggle to get through conceptual constraints.[7]

Freud's work, in this connection, should be read as in part at least an effort to make it possible to see things differently. His gift for making it possible through his examples and case studies for others to "see what I mean" is impressive. In fact a great amount of work in the social sciences does not involve hypothesis-testing even when it appears in that guise, but an effort by one or more, through the collection and organization of facts and proposals of explanations of them, to persuade others to see what they see.

Early rather than late in a science, there tends to be emphasis on winning agreement for the adoption of a domain, the adoption of a language in which to express the facts that will count, and the adoption of assumptions underlying procedures for making observations. An example

---

7. For an account of this process, see Hanson (1958, especially chapters 1 and 2).

is Freud's *Interpretation of Dreams*, which is a brilliant quintessentially "see-what-I-mean" book.

The notion of "intersubjective agreement," even "intersubjective agreement in principle" (when it is not practical for a number of people to make the same observation in the same place at the same time), assumes that not everyone can join in to make the verdict about whether or not an observation should be accepted. The agreement must be among those who are equally competent, who have equivalent knowledge of a domain and hypotheses about it. That is one reason apprenticeship and credentials are so important in science. Others, not on the jury, accept "on faith" the legitimacy of the jury verdict about an observation.[8]

Any science runs the risk that its experts will join to protect a theory or hypothesis rather than to challenge and thereby strengthen it. Therefore, science as an institution is determined to foster through a variety of sanctions the institutionalization of social norms that will mitigate this risk. There is no certain guarantee against the risk, which is why it must be guarded against. Indeed, the dilemma between conserving a theory or hypothesis that has proven itself over and over and continuing to challenge it becomes ever more painful in the history of any science.

In a group of experts, the strain is tolerable as long as its members see through the eyes of the same knowledge and accept the choice of domains to which this knowledge is held to be applicable.

However, all observations require interpretation.

> I now feel that I should have emphasized . . . the view that observations, and even more so observation statements and statements of experimental results, are always *interpretations* of the facts observed; that they are *interpretations in the light of theories*.[9] This is one of the main reasons why it is always deceptively easy to find *verifications* of a theory, and why we have to adopt a *highly critical* attitude towards our theories if we do not wish to argue in circles: the attitude of trying to refute them. [Popper, 1959a, p. 107n]

As soon as a member of the group begins to see things differently, to interpret phenomena differently, strain becomes apparent. Has the

---

8. Such faith, of course, is very difficult to maintain when there is as much disagreement as there appears to be among psychoanalysts when it comes to "interpreting" the data.

9. What Popper implies here—that the interpretation of the facts depends on the theory being tested—is not necessarily so. (See the distinction between nontheoretic and theoretic concepts in the discussion of the nonstatement view of theory, Part Two of this book.)

group member become a "quack," who is to be expelled because his observations are unreliable or do not make sense? Or is he the gifted herald of a new breakthrough?

The one who does not see the same things others do, or who makes sense of what others cannot make sense of, has the responsibility to define explicitly where the difference between him and them lies. Is he outside a domain shared with his colleagues, making statements about another domain? What knowledge not shared by them does he bring to bear upon observations?

If he cannot persuade others to join him in accepting his observations, if the decision is that in the light of accepted knowledge the observation does not make sense and is simply incapable of being "fitted in," then it may lie neglected, on the side of the road down which science proceeds, occasionally perhaps, with a change in shared knowledge, to be taken up again much later. An observation does not enter or change the body of scientific knowledge automatically—only as the result of a decision to accept it.

There is no use, then, in pretending that decisions in science are automatic, or that the results of even the most rigorous empirical tests are always clear-cut and unequivocal. The voluntaristic elements in science cannot be expunged—although an attempt may be made to regulate them—no matter how careful the logic or severe the methodological rules brought to bear.

However, science as a social institution regulates to some extent the choice of what the scientist is to question. Science is conservative. The greater the number of other rigorous empirical tests a hypothesis has previously survived, and, given such survival, the greater its content, scope, and precision compared to possible alternatives, the more warranted a scientist is to question his knowledge of the situation, the adequacy of his procedures, or the assumptions underlying his procedures, rather than to respond to an apparent falsification of his hypothesis by revising it or rejecting it altogether in favor of a competing alternative.

If a hypothesis is to be revised, rather than rejected in toto, generally a scientist will usually try to choose the minimal change in the hypothesis that will suffice to account for the falsifying observation as well as observations previously deduced in rigorous tests which the unrevised hypothesis did survive. However, a revision that accounts only for what is already known and does not lead to successful prediction of new unexpected observations is viciously ad hoc. On the basis of this criterion, we may conclude that Freud's revision of his theory in the face of the apparent falsification of what seems to be a universal generalization—"all dreams are wish-fulfillments"—to include the distinction between the manifest dream and the latent content of the dream is probably not viciously ad hoc.

Again it must be emphasized—here I have the debates about psychoanalytic theory, for example, in mind—that there is a wide range for discretion and error in making these choices. Often, there is no immediate way to judge where a choice will lead, how fruitful or sterile its consequences will be. The scientist must live with uncertainty and endless dilemmas. If he remains stubbornly committed to his hypothesis in the face of falsifications of it, he discredits himself and his field. On the other hand, if he quickly abandons it, he may prematurely and unnecessarily betray his own vision.

What is the status of the falsificationist view of science? To repeat briefly: Statements about observable phenomena do not entail or determine one and only one true explanation or hypothesis from which these statements can be deduced. There are always alternative possible worlds. Different sets of premises, different postulated properties or relations, any number of these possible worlds, might account for what the scientist discovers about phenomena. A scientist guesses which of these possible worlds is the actual world. He wants to say, if this were truly the way the world is, among all the ways it might be, then it follows that phenomena (or individuals in one or more domains) would be ordered, patterned, or related as he has discovered them to be, or that such-and-such a particular event will occur, fact will be true, or observation will be made.

A scientist tests his hypotheses by deducing different empirical consequences from alternative statements or sets of statements about the way the world is and seeing which consequences are true in the actual world. If such a consequence is a prediction or postdiction of something as yet unobserved or unknown, the rigor of the test is enhanced. The more precisely the rival consequences are stated, the smaller but more exact the difference between them, the more rigorous the test. That statement or set of statements about a possible world surviving, as other alternatives have not survived, all attempts to exclude it by this method as true of the actual world is adopted provisionally as so far, compared to any plausible rival, the better hypothesis. The scientist wants not so much to "confirm" hypotheses but rather in subjecting hypotheses to rigorous tests to exclude as many possibilities as he can.

Scientific method enters at the point a scientist deduces empirical consequences from hypotheses (conjoined with statements of specific conditions and auxiliary assumptions) about which possible worlds are excluded as "the actual world." He argues that, if a logical consequence of a hypothesis is shown empirically to be false, given the truth of statements about specific conditions and auxiliary assumptions, the hypothesis must be false.

Although if the logical consequence of a hypothesis is empirically true, the hypothesis is considered to have survived a test, there is no automatic procedure a scientist may follow warranting the conclusion that this hypothesis is part of, or is *the* true explanation. There is only a method a scientist may follow warranting the conclusion that, given some guesses, this hypothesis is a better guess than that.

Confirmation is not an acceptable criterion of demarcation of science from nonscience because no confirmation of a universal generalization is decisive and any observation statement is consistent with a number of different true and false universal generalizations. Falsification is not a completely adequate or satisfactory criterion of demarcation because science does not in fact constrain itself to automatic rejection of a hypothesis from which an observation statement that turns out to be empirically false has been deduced. A voluntaristic conception of science seems to fit both the logic and the history of science and its methods. It accepts that the scientist, in his quest for knowledge about the actual world, formulates hypotheses which are statements that exclude possibilities, regards such statements as corrigible, conducts rigorous empirical tests of them, and, confronted, as he inevitably is, by a number of choices, grants primacy to cognitive standards in making these choices, and in making choices takes risks about the future of his own work. Such are the aims and ideally the achievements of a distinctively scientific enterprise.

## 7. Psychoanalysis and the Challenge of Falsificationism

The view of science that, then, challenged psychoanalysis may be summarized briefly as follows. The criterion of falsifiability is designed to demarcate science in such a way that it avoids two problems. One is the underdetermination of theory by data. Any set of data can be deduced from, explained by, or held to "support," any number of theories. An instance of a hypothesis, which is at the same time an instance of rival or alternative hypotheses, cannot in itself decide between them. The second problem is the fact that no set of basic observation statements (data) logically entails a universal generalization.

A theory in this view is a set of sentences, whose form is characteristically that of a universal generalization. It is invented—a bold conjecture—not necessarily "induced" from data. (The problem of induction is rejected—induction in the sense of a logic for squeezing general truths from observations.) There are no constraints upon how a theory is to be invented. (The context of discovery is sharply distinguished from the context of justification.)

A theory excludes possibilities of what may be true of the world. The content of a theory is measured by the number of possibilities of what can be true of the world excluded by the theory. Because a universal generalization asserts what cannot possibly be true of the world, it can be decisively falsified by any instance of that which it claims cannot possibly be true.

A scientist subjects a theory to rigorous tests by deducing precise predictions from it (thus, the value of measurement). Such precision excludes a large number of possibilities. What is predicted is improbable (given background knowledge) and an in-this-sense improbable theory is of course vulnerable to falsification (an improbable outcome is not likely to occur).

If the prediction, which has been logically deduced from the theory, turns out to be false, if something that has been excluded as impossible turns out to the case, then the theory must by the laws of logic be false, and the scientist is morally bound to reject it. The scientist is not permitted, if he intends such tests to be rigorous, to rescue theories so falsified by ad hoc devices—appealing to unknown influences as responsible for an unwelcome result, questioning observations which would otherwise be held to be acceptable and error-free, or revising selected sentences of the theory just to fit the unwelcome finding.

Psychoanalytic theory is therefore criticized as follows.

1. Continuous effort is expended by adherents of the theory to immunize the theory against falsification rather than to test it. Adherents of the theory are reluctant to reject it even in the fact of apparently decisive falsifications (for example, the apparent falsification of the wish-fulfillment theory of dreams by instances of disagreeable dreams).[10] They carry out ad hoc rescues of it. These adherents' determination to immunize the theory against falsification results in sterile appeal to authority, lack of progressive accumulation of knowledge, and unresponsiveness to new findings.

2. The theory itself is in principle not falsifiable. It does not exclude

---

10. Freud did in fact revise the wish-fulfillment theory of dreams in view of the counterexamples provided by traumatic dreams.

any possibilities (no evidence makes any difference). Its predictions are insufficiently precise to make rigorous testing of it possible.[11]

But the falsificationist's view of theory can also be questioned. The reluctance of psychoanalysts to abandon psychoanalytic theory in the face of apparent falsifications has been observed to be common in "normal science." One has only to think of the convinced, committed researcher who revises and repeats an experiment over and over until it "comes out right." Furthermore, it is not clear that change in science occurs as a result of the ruthless rejections of theories in the face of apparent falsifications (Kuhn, 1970).

On the nonstatement view of theory, a theory is a tool used to solve problems or explain facts in different domains. Every scientific theory appears to have a core which in a particular domain or set of domains has had resounding success and which is therefore relatively immune to falsification; and from this core, by the addition of special laws, the theory extends into other domains where it may or may not be so successful. If when it is so extended it fails, such a single failure in and of itself is not enough to justify its abandonment. Only when a theory outlives its usefulness—repeatedly failing when extended to new domains, and thus manifesting a limited capacity for such extension—is it dislodged by another theory, and then only by a theory that can do everything it can do and more. One does not throw away a tool unless one has a better one, or reject a shelter with a leaky roof for no shelter at all (Kuhn, 1970; Stegmüller, 1976).[12]

That psychoanalytic propositions are not in principle nonfalsifiable has been argued at length. (In addition, Grünbaum, whose critique of Popper's position is the most telling, comments quite rightly on Popper's "misdepiction" of psychoanalytic theory.)

A falsificationist may claim (on the basis of what often appears to be superficial knowledge of psychoanalysis) that in psychoanalysis the same observation can be argued to be consistent with both a hypothesis and the contradictory of that hypothesis, or that an observation state-

11. A distinction should be made between the first set of criticisms, which are directed at putative regrettable failings of adherents of the theory, and this set of criticisms, which are directed at the theory itself.

12. This emphasis does not make the nonstatement view of theory an instrumental one focused only on the utility of a theory and not on its truth. A theoretical hypothesis, in the nonstatement view of theory, makes an empirical claim about a domain (the claim that a theoretical predicate is true of it); and this claim is provisionally accepted as true or false "on the evidence."

ment and its contradictory can both be held to be consistent with the truth of the same hypothesis. Therefore, no hypothesis can be falsified by observation.

This criticism is usually based on a false assumption, namely, that some logical disjunction (either this or that) is an exhaustive disjunction of the possibilities. While it is true, for example, that neither extremely affectionate solicitous behavior nor unfriendly behavior may falsify a hypothesis of unconscious hostility toward father, appropriate filial affection or indifference could conceivably do so (Salmon, 1959).

In addition, there are many kinds of facts which are relevant to any such hypothesis, and a combination of such facts may disconfirm the hypothesis (confirm its "negative"). As Salmon points out, a variety of independent evidence is available to the investigator: how an individual deals with hostility in many situations, whether situations arousing conscious anger in others arouse conscious anger in this individual, what this individual dreams, what kind of parapraxes this individual commits under what circumstances. There is nothing impermissible in the use of the same behavior (for example, a smile) to count as confirming two different (even contradictory) hypotheses (for example, friendliness or covert hostility), since the confirmation depends not on the smile alone but on what the other facts are (Hospers, 1959).

When Freud observed that some dreams occur which do not appear to be wish-fulfillments, and interpreted these dreams nevertheless to be wish-fulfillments—that is, fulfillments of a wish to refute his theory—the interpretation does seem designed to block falsification of his generalization that all dreams are wish-fulfillments.[13] However, the possibility that other facts may exist, which are capable of "disconfirming" this interpretation, argues that this interpretation is not simply an ad hoc rescue of the generalization. Someone might dream such a dream who has never heard of Freud's theory, who has given no independent evidence of being negatively disposed toward Freud's theory (has not heard about the theory for the first time or is not in analysis and experiencing strong resistance), or whose experiences during the day prior to the dream did not include a consideration of Freud's theory. These facts, if true, constitute evidence which at the least would count against acceptance of the interpretation (Salmon, 1959).

13. Freud also uses the distinction between manifest and latent content to argue that apparent counterexamples to this generalization are not actual counterexamples. (I have already suggested that this argument is not viciously ad hoc, since the distinction appears to be explanatory in other independent contexts.)

Although some disagreements about interpretations are dismissed as "resistance," thus apparently fortifying psychoanalytic propositions from falsification, "there are plenty of situations in which an interpretation is attacked and no psychoanalyst would say that the attacker was 'resisting.'" In addition, that individuals respond with impassioned rejection "when the truth hurts" is a generalization from experience, not, as some philosophers of science apparently assume, an a priori dictum (Hospers, 1959).

Glymour and Grünbaum both remind us that psychoanalytic hypotheses have in fact been falsified. Glymour attributes Freud's rejection of the etiologic role of actual events in favor of the etiologic role of "psychic reality" to his failure to confirm a prediction in the case of the Rat Man. That the Rat Man's father actually punished him for masturbating was predicted from psychoanalytic hypotheses. The prediction turned out to be false (at least, there was no evidence it was true). The revision of etiologic hypotheses so falsified was required, and in fact such hypotheses were revised by Freud. Grünbaum also points out that "Freud's repeated *modifications* of his theories were clearly motivated by evidence . . ." (1979, p. 135). An important example is the rejection of the seduction hypothesis to account for neurosis.

In addition, Grünbaum reminds us that "Freud's theory contains causal hypotheses of a developmental and etiological sort, and . . . at least some of these causal hypotheses are, in principle, falsifiable by *controlled* inquiry . . ." (1977b, p. 347). Examples of falsifiable assertions include that such traits as orderliness, parsimony, and obstinacy are correlated, and that the etiology of such a cluster of traits is to be found in specified unfavorable infantile experiences.

# 3     Can Evidence Obtained in the Psychoanalytic Situation Test Psychoanalytic Hypotheses?

The answer Grünbaum (1977a, 1977b, 1978, 1979, 1980, 1981, 1982a, 1982b) gives to the question "Can theoretical hypotheses be tested in the psychoanalytic situation?" in a series of important and provocative papers is "No."[1] This conclusion, which presupposes the canons of eliminative inductivism, appears to be based in large part upon the following considerations. First, Freud and other psycho-analysts once relied upon the so-called tally argument to justify drawing upon clinical evidence to support psychoanalytic hypotheses, but were forced over time to abandon this argument. (The tally argument takes as a premise that interpretations owe their therapeutic efficacy to the fact they they tally with what is true.)[2] Second, the data (the analysand's reports) that are obtained in the psychoanalytic situation are unavoid-ably corrupted both by the psychoanalyst's (unwitting) suggestions and by the analysand's own prior knowledge and theoretical preconceptions.

This corruption is the problem addressed recently, especially with re-gard to testing hypotheses about the past, by Spence (1982). Just four years earlier, Spence and his coauthor Luborsky, both gifted empirical investigators, wrote a cautiously optimistic review of the status of quan-titative research on psychoanalytic therapy (Luborsky and Spence, 1978). Now, disturbingly enough, Spence writes in a vein suggesting he has joined others (for example, those who classify psychoanalysis as a hermeneutic rather than a scientific discipline) in concluding that objec-tive truth even about a single patient may not be obtainable in psycho-analysis. Instead, what is effective in a particular clinical instance of psychoanalytic therapy is narrative "truth" (what is merely possible and acceptable on aesthetic or hedonic grounds to psychoanalyst and analysand). But this narrative "truth" does not necessarily correspond, and cannot be shown to correspond, to the actual world as it is; it does

1. J. Edelson first brought this work to my attention in a personal communication.
2. I shall state the tally argument in full in section 5 of this chapter, p. 47.

not claim to be knowledge of the actual world; and it "fits" one set of data only (it is not general or generalizable).

## 1. Eliminative Inductivism and Falsificationism

Eliminative inductivism answers the question "What evidence shall count as *scientific support* for a hypothesis?" in a way that distinguishes it from the enumerative inductivism associated with logical positivism and from Popper's falsificationism. In brief, enumerative inductivism holds that any positive instance of a hypothesis—any observation entailed by it or deducible from it—confirms it. Falsificationism holds that the survival by a hypothesis, which is capable of being falsified, of a rigorous attempt empirically to falsify it contributes to the degree to which it is regarded as corroborated. Grünbaum emphasizes that psychoanalytic hypotheses are confirmable and falsifiable, and that the significance of this claim about them is not as great as some think.

Grünbaum exaggerates, perhaps, the difference between falsificationism and eliminative inductivism. The canons of eliminative inductivism could be taken as an elaboration of what Popper means by "a rigorous test of a hypothesis." Indeed, I am inclined to regard these canons as a specification of what is meant by scientific reasoning. Falsificationism and eliminative inductivism, in fact, do not represent different views of science. They are responses to different questions. Popper asks, "What qualifies a statement as worthy of any attention at all from scientists?" He answers, "That it is falsifiable." Among such falsifiable statements, some will survive and continue to survive rigorous tests in a general competition with rivals. Eliminative inductivism is a response rather to the question "What makes a statement, which science has accepted as scientifically meaningful, scientifically credible?" The emphasis on achieving the status of scientific credibility rather than the status of "candidate for the status of scientific credibility," and on obtaining evidence that supports a hypothesis over specific rival and multiple alternative hypotheses, does serve, however, to distinguish eliminative inductivism from falsificationism.

What follows is my own version (enlarging on Grünbaum's) of a stringent formulation of the canons of eliminative inductivism. This formulation, especially the fourth canon, makes explicit the dependence of eliminative inductivism in general on a notion of comparative support. Support is a comparative, not an absolute, concept. The support which evidence provides a hypothesis is always relative to the support the same evidence provides another rival or alternative hypothesis. Evidence supports a hypothesis if it not only confirms the hypothesis but refutes, fails to confirm, or gives much much less support to rival or alternative hypotheses. Evidence which is capable of supporting a hypothesis is probative—that is, tests the hypothesis. Merely confirming instances of a hypothesis as such cannot be probative.

## 2. The Canons of Eliminative Inductivism

An observable outcome of an experiment, or of some process, set-up, or arrangement in nature, counts as probative evidence in support of a hypothesis about a domain, if the following statements are true.

### The First Canon

The outcome is deducible, or follows logically, from the hypothesis. If the hypothesis is true, then the outcome must occur (the occurence of the outcome is a necessary—although not a sufficient—condition for the truth of the hypothesis); or, if the hypothesis is probabilistic, then the process, set-up, or arrangement has a much much greater propensity to produce the outcome than it would have if the hypothesis were false. In other words, the criterion of confirmability has been met by the hypothesis. However, the outcome does not qualify as support for the hypothesis just because it confirms or is a positive instance of the hypothesis.

### The Second Canon

The outcome is predicted on the basis of knowledge of the hypothesis before it has actually been observed. On the basis of what is already known (background knowledge), and without knowledge of the hypothesis, the outcome's occurrence would not have been predicted, or its failure to occur would have been predicted; its occurrence is, therefore, unexpected.

### The Third Canon

The outcome occurs. It must be possible that the outcome might not have occurred, so that the hypothesis could and would have been falsified had the outcome failed to occur. But as it turns out, the hypothesis is not falsified. The criterion of falsifiability has been met by the hypothesis, but the outcome does not qualify as support for the hypothesis, just because the hypothesis is falsifiable (although not actually falsified).

## The Fourth Canon

The hypothesis—which here I call $H_1$—has at least one rival, a hypothesis $H_2$, which is about the same domain. The outcome warrants provisional acceptance of the hypothesis $H_1$ as true of the domain *over the rival hypothesis $H_2$*, on at least *one* of the following grounds. (At least one of three possible relations between the hypotheses $H_1$ and $H_2$ holds.)

*a*) The outcome is incompatible with (falsifies) the rival hypothesis $H_2$. (That the outcome will not occur is deducible from the rival hypothesis $H_2$.) [3] Or:

*b*) Neither the occurrence of the outcome nor its failure to occur is deducible from the rival hypothesis $H_2$. (The rival hypothesis $H_2$ has nothing to say about the outcome.) Or:

*c*) Given the truth of the rival hypothesis $H_2$, the occurrence of the

---

3. The hypotheses $H_1$ and $H_2$ of course can involve the same set of variables, but their claims will differ then, for example, with respect to: (*a*) whether or not some variables are related at all, (*b*) the kind of relation that exists between or among the variables, or (*c*) how strong the relation between them is.

In this case, the hypotheses $H_1$ and $H_2$ are rivals *within* a particular theoretical framework (the usual situation in science). Philosophers of science should distinguish more often than they do between this situation and that in which *two theoretical frameworks* are competing. What goes into a decision to prefer one theoretical framework over another is not necessarily identical with what goes into a decision to prefer one hypothesis over another within the same theoretical framework.

I have not attempted to make or keep consistently to such a distinction, because it would require what in this book would be an extensive digression into matters far afield. I shall simply indicate here for the interested reader that making the distinction involves, in the framework of the nonstatement view of theory (see Part Two), the difference between competing theoretical predicates and rival hypotheses. So, we have the difference between competing theories of dreams, a psychoanalytic theory and nonpsychoanalytic theory, on the one hand, and between two rival psychoanalytic hypotheses about dreams, on the other.

Theoretical hypotheses using different theoretical predicates may make different, competing but not necessarily incompatible, claims as to what kind of system a domain in a set of domains is. But incompatible hypotheses about the relations in a domain between or among a selected set of concepts or variables are rivals—one or the other but not both can be used to define a theoretical predicate, which is intended to be applied to a particular kind of system. The theoretical predicate is true of that kind of system just because a set of such hypotheses is true of it. Rival hypotheses are different answers to the question, "What are the relationships between just these concepts or variables in a domain that is supposed to be a particular kind of system?"

outcome is not simply rarer or more unexpected but much much rarer, much much more unexpected, than if the hypothesis $H_1$ were true. This possible relation between rival hypotheses has been explicated by Hacking (1965). Hacking's formulation of a premise of comparative support may be paraphrased as follows.

IF an observation statement describes an actual outcome, which is one member of a set of possible outcomes;

and that observation statement is consistent with the truth of any one of a set of rival hypotheses, although each one of these hypotheses assigns different probabilities to the possible outcomes (each hypothesis entails a different probability distribution for the set of possible outcomes);

and given the truth of one hypothesis the actual outcome is assigned a much much greater probability than it would be assigned given the truth of some rival hypothesis;

THEN provisional acceptance of this one hypothesis instead of the rival hypothesis is justified (the one is not simply better but far far better supported by the evidence than the other).

## The Fifth Canon

The plan for observing or obtaining the outcome is such that a convincing argument for eliminating plausible alternative explanations (other than the truth of the hypothesis $H_1$) for the occurrence of the outcome, should it occur, can be made from examining the outcome and the way in which the outcome is obtained. Some of these alternative explanations may seem both possible and plausible in one study after another, and may be in any particular study more or less extraneous to the investigator's focal interests. (They are not necessarily within his theoretical framework.) Such alternative explanations propose what variables might have acted to bring about the occurrence of the outcome, even though the hypothesis $H_1$ be false, had their influence not been excluded or controlled.

## The Sixth Canon

The plan for observing or obtaining the outcome is such that a convincing argument for eliminating plausible alternative explanations (other than the falsity of the hypothesis $H_1$) for the failure of the outcome to occur, should it not occur, can be made from examining whatever other outcome does occur and the way in which that outcome is obtained. These alternative explanations (some of which may seem plausible in study after study, and may be in any particular study more or less extraneous to the investigator's focal interests) propose what variables might have acted to prevent the occurrence of the outcome, even though the hypothesis $H_1$ be true, had their influence not been excluded or controlled. (Clearly, then, there will be cases—certainly so, when it is not possible to exclude even all known plausible alternative explanations for the failure of a predicted outcome to occur—such that an apparent falsification of the hypothesis $H_1$ cannot be regarded as conclusive.)

It is clear from the statement of these six canons that hypotheses can only be provisionally accepted as true, relative to the time of their testing, and to whatever specific rival hypotheses and plausible alternative explanations are available and eliminated at the time of testing. For the set of rival hypotheses about a domain, and the set of the plausible alternative explanations for the occurrence, or failure to occur, of an outcome, are infinite; and future members of these sets, which come into being in part as the result of the acquisition of new knowledge, are unforeseeable.

## 3. Psychoanalytic Hypotheses Cannot be Tested in the Pyschoanalytic Situation

Grünbaum takes four major steps to argue that, while psychoanalytic hypotheses may be falsifiable, they have not achieved scientific credibility from data obtained outside the psychoanalytic situation and cannot achieve such credibility from data obtained in the psychoanalytic situation. One, he points to the current unavailability of, and lack of interest by psychoanalysts in, experimental evidence. Two, he shows that Freud and others depended upon the so-called tally argument for establishing the credibility of psychoanalytic hypotheses nonexperimentally. Three, he claims that, because of the inability of psychoanalytic clinical investigators to meet the requirements of the canons of eliminative inductivism, Freud and others have gradually had to abandon the tally argument. Four, he examines the data available in the psychoanalytic situation and concludes that these data are unavoidably corrupted by the psychoanalyst's (unwitting) suggestions and selection biases, the analysand's own prior knowledge and theoretical preconceptions, and the fallibility of the analysand's memory and his reasoning about his own experience, and therefore cannot be used independently of the tally argument to support psychoanalytic hypotheses according to the canons of eliminative inductivism.[4]

## 4. Experimental Evidence

Grünbaum's argument begins with the observation that experimental evidence, providing support according to the canons of eliminative inductivism for psychoanalytic theory, has not been forthcoming. Freud and other psychoanalysts have claimed they do not need support from this source, because of the clinical observations available to them.[5] Furthermore, psychoanalysts have tended to regard failure here as inevitable, because phenomena to which the psychoanalyst has access in the psychoanalytic situation are simply not available in experimental situations.

## 5. The Tally Argument

That Freud and other psychoanalysts feel they can give such weight to clinical observations depends ultimately, according to Grünbaum, upon the tally argument.[6]

I am not clear whether Grünbaum in his statement and discussion of the tally argument always distinguishes between interpretations (hypotheses which are more or less general statements about the analysand) and general theoretical psychoanalytic hypotheses—or, for that matter, between interpretations that attribute some property, state, or attitude to the analysand, and interpretations that purport to explain causally some state, attitude, production, symptom, or other aspect of the analysand.

4. In this chapter I shall paraphrase Grünbaum's argument. Here, for the most part, I do not take a position about the points he makes, or adduce evidence or quote from the literature to support or raise questions about his assertions. I shall indicate in Part Two of this book what is necessary for a complete response to his argument, and I shall respond to his argument in considerable detail in Part Three. The reader who wishes to have a more complete statement of Grünbaum's argument, along with an account of the literature he cites in support of it, should consult his papers.

5. "I have examined your experimental studies for the verification of the psychoanalytic assertions with interest. I cannot put much value on these confirmations because the wealth of reliable observations on which these assertions rest make them independent of experimental verification" (Freud, quoted by Luborsky and Spence, 1978, pp. 356–357).

6. "After all, [the analysand's] conflicts will only be successfully solved and his resistances overcome if the anticipatory ideas [interpretations] he is given tally with what is real in him. Whatever in the doctor's conjectures is inaccurate drops out in the course of the analysis; it has to be withdrawn and replaced by something more correct" (Freud, 1916–1917, p. 452).

Frequently, he seems to refer to causal interpretations, but treats these as if they were identical with the general theoretical propositions of psychoanalysis. In order to avoid complicating the paraphrase of his argument and my response to this argument, I have not insisted on these distinctions here.

In fact, I shall hold throughout that a psychoanalytic interpretation, frequently, is a hypothesis about the analysand—a supposition about a state of affairs (subjective or situational) in which the analysand is a participant. Such an interpretation follows or is logically entailed by one or more nontheoretic facts (what the analysand reports, or that he reports what he reports) in conjunction with at least one psychoanalytic theoretic hypothesis. Support for an interpretation depends in part upon whether a chain of similar entailments, involving other facts and hypotheses, converge independently upon the same interpretation.

I do not mean to imply by this formulation that the psychoanalyst in the clinical situation is wittingly making logical deductions to arrive at an interpretation. The psychoanalyst may arrive at his interpretation in many ways (here, he is in the context of discovery and not in the context of justification)—for example, through preconscious mental processes, which are influenced by empathic identification with or reciprocal signal-responses to the analysand's activity. Justifying provisional acceptance of a hypothesis, however, requires a formal statement of its relation to evidence. Still, according to Glymour (1980), Freud's Rat Man case (which I shall consider in Part Three of this book) shows Freud interpreting nontheoretic facts (for example, the analysand's reports of his states and attitudes) by making inferences from a conjunction of these reports and psychoanalytic theoretical hypotheses.

The tally argument has the following form (I have altered Grünbaum's presentation somewhat):

*a*) *Premise 1.* Psychoanalytic therapy is successful only if the analysand achieves veridical insight (not pseudoinsight but objectively true knowledge of himself), and he achieves veridical insight only if the interpretations of the psychoanalyst tally with what is objectively true.

*b*) *Premise 2.* Psychoanalytic therapy is successful.

*c*) *Conclusion.* Therefore, the analysand achieves veridical insight—and so psychoanalytic interpretations do not only *seem* true to the analysand (that is, such interpretations are not simply regarded by the analysand as plausible or—as those who regard psychoanalysis as hermeneutics would say—as meaningful), but psychoanalytic interpretations are objectively true as well. (And, therefore, I would add, the general theoretical hypotheses of psychoanalysis which yield these interpretations have survived a test which might have resulted in their refutation.)

Grünbaum does not make explicit what he implies in the first premise—that whether interpretations tally with what is true of the analysand will determine assessment of the truth-value of general theoretical hypotheses of psychoanalysis to which these interpretations are logically related. So, if an inference (interpretation) is false, then the general theoretical hypothesis or the report by the analysand of his states and attitudes (for example, what he consciously believes, wishes, or perceives), or both, from the conjunction of which the interpretation was inferred, must be false. The general theoretical hypothesis is tested by predicting from it in conjunction with one or more facts that an interpretation (a statement about the analysand) is true. It is, therefore, important to have some outcome—such as therapeutic effect—which logically follows from a true interpretation, in order to evaluate in turn whether the interpretation (the hypothesis about the analysand) can be accepted as true.

The tally argument takes the correspondence theory of truth for granted. Freud does allude to and at times wrestle with the problems of demonstrating that a statement corresponds to a factual state of affairs (Edelson, 1976), but on the whole formulations presupposing the correspondence theory of truth accord with the naive realism which, I might say inevitably, was part of his conceptual equipment as a scientist.

## 6. Abandonment of the Tally Argument

However, Grünbaum proceeds, the tally argument has had to be abandoned. Spence (1982, pp. 289–290) traces Freud's move away from "reconstruction" (recapturing memories, which tally with interpretations) to "construction" (Freud, 1937); I believe he is mistaken in concluding, on these grounds, that failure of the tally argument functions for Grünbaum as a straw man. It is precisely the implications for psychoanalysis of its own abandonment of the tally argument as a basis for warranting psychoanalytic hypotheses as scientifically credible that Grünbaum is exploring. Spence's own move away from a focus on historical truth (which is true or false of the actual world) to a focus on narrative "truth" (which is therapeutically effective or ineffective) may itself be in part a consequence of the abandonment by Freud and others of the tally argument. Current interest in the proposal to regard psychoanalysis as hermeneutics (as purveying subjective or narrative "truth" rather than objective truth) has arisen, it seems to me, as confidence in the tally argument has increasingly been eroded, in the absence of any sense of what evidence obtainable in the psychoanalytic situation might replace therapeutic outcome to justify provisional acceptance of psychoanalytic interpretations as objectively true.

Here is a summary of Grünbaum's account of the abandonment of the tally argument.

*a*) This argument had its most convincing exemplification in such cases as Breuer's Anna O. (Breuer and Freud, 1893–1895, pp. 21–47). That the "talking cure," leading to recovery of the memory of a traumatic event, seemed to be effective in removing symptoms was used to argue that the hypothesis is true that repression is a necessary condition for the development of—and, therefore, a specific etiology of—such symptoms. Evidence is needed, of course, to support that it is just this specific feature of the treatment—talking, which leads to recovery of a repressed memory—and not some other aspect of the treatment (the relationship with the physician, for example) which is responsible for the disappearance of the symptoms. Such evidence was apparently obtained; the treatment was able to cause the disappearance of each symptom separately, without influencing other symptoms. This result tends to support the hypothesis that it is the recovery of the repressed memory—rather than the hypothesis that it is some general or inadvertent agent—which is responsible for the outcome of treatment.

*b*) However, the treatment effect was unreliable. Symptoms did not remain in remission. Instead, they recurred, apparently depending, according to Freud, upon the vicissitudes of the patient-physician relationship. In order to be able to account for the unreliability of outcome and continue to claim that the specific etiology of such symptoms is repression, Freud moved the past event even further backward in time. It is not repression of a recent traumatic event but of a childhood memory which is the etiologic agent. This extrapolation, however, does not have a convincing exemplification, such as would have been provided by the *independent* mitigation of different symptoms in such cases as Anna O., had that mitigation proved reliable.

*c*) There is no evidence to support, according to the canons of eliminative inductivism, the first premise of the tally argument (that therapy is successful only if the interpretations are true). Suppose we disregard the increasingly accepted fact that life events and maturation itself may have profound "therapeutic" effects, and are rival explanations of any therapeutic outcome. Suppose we also accept that the outcome of psychoanalytic therapy is better than the outcome that would have resulted from those influences that might have affected the patient if he had had no therapy at all. There is still no evidence supporting the hypothesis that veridical insights, effected by veridical interpretations, are necessary to achieve a presumed successful outcome of psychoanalysis. There is no evidence eliminating the possibility that other aspects of psychoanalytic therapy are responsible for its outcome, and no evidence that such an outcome is not achieved as well by other rival therapies, which relying on other means make no use of such interpretations.

So, even if the outcome of psychoanalytic therapy is better than that which would be expected to occur "spontaneously," there is no evidence which, by ruling out other plausible possible causes of such an outcome, supports the hypothesis that veridical psychoanalytic interpretations are responsible for it. Other possible causes include: (1) unwitting suggestion by the psychoanalyst (in the form of nonveridical or pseudoexplanations); (2) the belief of psychoanalyst and analysand in the truth and efficacy of the psychoanalyst's interpretations (inadvertent placebo effect); or (3) aspects of the psychoanalytic situation other than veridical interpretations (for example, the analysand experiences a new kind of relationship with the psychoanalyst), which aspects may, in fact, be the intended rather than inadvertent agents of change in other therapies.[7]

Symptoms have been removed by other therapies, apparently permanently and without substitution of other symptoms. When psychoanalysts account for this by supposing that symptoms so affected by other therapies are "ghost" symptoms which have achieved autonomy (are no longer connected to an active conflict), they have, unwittingly perhaps, undercut the argument that remission of symptoms through undoing of repression is evidence for the hypothesis that an active unconscious conflict is a necessary condition for the presence of a symptom and, therefore, that a prior repression is etiologically necessary for its having developed in the first place.

*d*) There is no evidence to support, according to the canons of eliminative inductivism, even the second premise of the tally argument (that psychoanalytic therapy is successful). In the absence of prior knowl-

---

7. Grünbaum does not add that psychoanalysts have not provided evidence eliminating the possibility that other aspects of the psychoanalytic situation might enable the analysand to achieve veridical insight even in the absence of interpretations (strictly defined) made by the psychoanalyst.

edge of the propensity of different neuroses to spontaneous remission, which is unavailable, a comparison of the effects of "psychoanalytic therapy" with the effects of "no formal treatment" (that is, the effects of life events and maturation, for example) upon similar patients (especially similar with respect to suitability for psychoanalytic treatment), who have the same kind and severity of illness, is required but has not been forthcoming.

*e*) The evidence required is difficult to impossible to obtain. The effects of interpretations are irretrievably and inseparably confounded in the psychoanalytic situation with inadvertent placebo effect and suggestion.

*f*) Therefore, Grünbaum concludes, the tally argument cannot be used to claim that psychoanalytic hypotheses have been or can be tested in the psychoanalytic situation.

## 7. Data Obtained in the Pyschoanalytic Situation

In conclusion, Grünbaum goes on to ask, if the tally argument fails, what evidence other than therapeutic effect can the psychoanalyst obtain in the psychoanalytic situation that would justify provisional acceptance of any psychoanalytic hypothesis over a rival hypothesis?

*a*) Some have taken the position that unexpected statistical associations can be predicted from psychoanalytic theory and then observed in the psychoanalytic situation. Others have been impressed by the convergence of conclusions derived from analysis of symptoms, dreams, and parapraxes. These means of testing psychoanalytic hypotheses in the psychoanalytic situation are unacceptable, according to Grünbaum, because there is no way to eliminate, given the nature of the method of free association, alternative plausible explanations of such statistical associations and convergences.

That conclusions arrived at from analysis of symptoms, dreams, and parapraxes converge does not constitute evidential support for them, because the apparently different data are not really independent; they are all obtained by the same method, free association. Statistical correlations are also based on data obtained by the method of free association, but Grünbaum claims that this method yields probatively defective, contaminated data. There is no way, in other words, of eliminating extraneous influences or adulterants, which provide plausible alternative explanations for a convergence or correlation.

*b*) Data yielded by free association are contaminated by the following influences.

(1) These data may result from the inadvertent influence exerted by

the psychoanalyst. Unwittingly, he conveys nonverbal or paraverbal cues; he chooses when in the course of free association to remain silent and when to interrupt; he chooses when to ask and when not to ask for associations or for further associations.

(2) The psychoanalyst's own selection biases may determine, especially in the absence of any prior criteria, which associations he uses and weaves together, and which he ignores, in arriving at an interpretation.

(3) The analysand may be led, by his own prior knowledge of psychoanalysis and by his own beliefs about what is expected by the psychoanalyst, to produce these statistical relationships and convergent conclusions.

*c*) Any response of the analysand's to interpretations (other than therapeutic outcome)—for example, assent to an interpretation previously resisted, or recovery of a memory—is also nonprobative (cannot be used to support psychoanalytic hypotheses), because it is impossible to eliminate as explanatory candidates the following possible causes of these responses.

(1) They may be determined by the psychoanalyst's witting or unwitting suggestions.

(2) They may be determined by the analysand's own theoretical preconceptions (not necessarily independent of psychoanalytic theory) about his introspections.

(3) They may be determined by the analysand's logically fallacious inferences concerning the reasons and causes of his states and attitudes. He may, for example, attribute causal relevance to contents, because one follows another, when no such attribution is logically warranted. Introspection gives no direct, privileged access to objectively true knowledge of reasons and causes.

(4) Memories, especially, are untrustworthy. Fictitious events are "remembered" as having occurred. Memories are constructions, not mere registrations.[8] Confabulations enter into what is remembered.

(5) Both assent and rejection following an interpretation cannot be taken at face value, but can only be evaluated in the light of new associations, including new memories, or, for example, a report that a symptom is aggravated. These data, in turn, also suffer from the defects previously mentioned.

*d*) Finally, Grünbaum rejects the presumption of the causal role of

---

8. A good discussion of the constructive aspect of memory, and indeed of the role of recovered memories in psychoanalytic treatment, can be found in E. Kris (1956b).

repression, which apparently provides warrant for inferences from free association.

(1) That presumption, as previously noted by him in connection with the collapse of the tally argument, itself lacks warrant. Since it does not hold up even for the neuroses, its extrapolation from neuroses to dreams and parapraxes is also unwarranted, making even clearer the dubious evidential value of the fact that conclusions derived from analysis of symptoms, dreams, and parapraxes converge.

(2) That an analysand has an association to some content does not warrant the conclusion that the association is causally related to that content. Even if one could support from free associations the hypothesis that a particular childhood event did occur and was then repressed (and it seems unlikely one could), the existence of that event does not support the hypothesis that the repressed event is causally (etiologically) relevant to an adult neurosis. For there is no way to show from the free associations of any analysand that the symptom would have developed only in case the event occurred and was repressed, and that therefore if the event had not occurred and/or had not been repressed the symptom would not have developed.[9] For the support of such etiological hypotheses, extraclinical evidence from prospective studies, where manipulation of the causative factor is possible, is clearly required.[10]

9. One does not need to assume at this point in Grünbaum's argument that the event is an external or situational rather than internal or subjective event.

10. An impressive—the best and most complete—statement of his position and this argument, as of this writing, will be found in Grünbaum (1982b). It includes both an appreciation of Freud as a scientist and methodologist, and a trenchant analysis of the problems involved in the claim that psychoanalytic hypotheses can be tested in the psychoanalytic situation.

# PART 2

# Preparing to Respond

What does psychoanalysis need to be able to do in order to respond effectively to the challenge of eliminative inductivism?

First, psychoanalysis must find ways of improving the presently poor quality of reasoning about the relation between hypothesis and evidence in its single case studies. Grünbaum appears to equate eliminative inductivism with one method of satisfying its canons. Group-comparison research is that method, but it is not without its own difficulties and infelicities; and it is unlikely that psychoanalysts will ever devote themselves in a major way to testing psychoanalytic hypotheses in experimental research involving comparison of groups of subjects, each group representing a different treatment, condition, or different level of a treatment. A growing literature on single subject research as an alternative to group-comparison research awaits exploration by psychoanalysts. This literature describes ways to achieve validity and generalizability in experimental and nonexperimental, quantitative and qualitative, statistical and nonstatistical, single subject research.

Second, the stubborn neglect of probability theory by psychoanalysis should come to an end—especially in view of the long time span presupposed by many psychoanalytic hypotheses between distal cause (or necessary condition) and effect; and the many known and unknown variables operating to influence causal relations in the domain(s) of interest to psychoanalysis. In addition, probabilistic statements not only may be necessary to express or compensate for the ignorance of the investigator by estimating how much an outcome can be attributed to uncontrolled or extraneous variables, but may capture as well some intrinsic feature of the phenomena he studies. For example, a process, arrangement, or set-up may possess (as an intrinsic property) different propensities, under a given condition, to display each of the possible outcomes of that process, arrangement, or set-up.

Many psychoanalytic "laws" (assuming such laws can eventually be formulated) will best be stated probabilistically rather than nonprobabilistically; "causality" or "psychic" determinism, on the one hand, and "probability," on the other, are not terms in contradictions (Suppes, 1970). Indeed, there is a new way of interpreting probability—as an objective propensity of a single case—which enhances more than ever the suitability of using the theory of probability in the single subject research upon which psychoanalysis, for the most part, must depend. The use of the theory of probability, required, for example, in reasoning statistically about the relation between hypothesis and evidence in at least some single subject studies the like of which might be carried out by psychoanalytic investigators, becomes meaningful when a hypothesis asserts that a single case under certain conditions has an objective propensity of a certain strength (which is a property of it) to display a particular kind of action, or asserts that with a change in conditions the strength of such a propensity changes.

Third, psychoanalytic theory itself should be clarified, for it is not clear to me that those like Grünbaum who write about it have the same things in mind I (or one or another group of psychoanalysts) have in mind. In any attempt to clarify the psychoanalytic theory that is to be tested, the following questions will have to be addressed. What is the domain investigated? What are the facts of interest in this domain? How are these to be explained by psychoanalytic theory? What does the term "psychoanalytic theory" designate? What is included in or encompassed by it? What parts of it are central, and what parts peripheral? Do some parts of it have more evidential support than others?

Fourth, the effort to formulate psychoanalytic theory more rigorously will inevitably come up against issues associated with the ancient mind-body problem. Some of the questions requiring answers here are: Is psychoanalytic theory ultimately a theory of the brain? Does psychoanalysis depend upon the neural sciences for testing its hypotheses according to the canons of eliminative inductivism? Is work in the neural sciences, then, capable of falsifying, casting doubt upon, or forcing re-vision of psychoanalytic hypotheses about the mind?

I believe both sets of questions can best be tackled in the framework of the nonstatement view of theory.

# 4  Psychoanalysis and Single Subject Research

       If adherence to the canons of eliminative inductivism is viewed as dependent upon comparing *groups of subjects*—with each group representing a different treatment, condition, or level of a treatment—then clearly psychoanalytic hypotheses cannot be tested in the psychoanalytic situation. But such a view confuses these canons with one concrete method for adhering to them in practice. Psychoanalysts must be prepared to argue that adherence to the canons of eliminative inductivism is to varying degrees possible in single subject research. At the same time, if psychoanalytic single case studies are intended to make empirical claims and to justify these claims as scientifically credible, psychoanalysts must work toward bringing such studies into conformity with these canons.

There are problems in achieving these objectives. The mention of single subject research is apt to arouse a snigger from investigators (and readers for and editors of scientific journals) in psychiatry, who identify it with what Campbell and Stanley (1963) call "the one-shot case study." This kind of study, typified by many narrative case histories and accounts of treatment in psychoanalysis, does not exclude any plausible alternative hypotheses that might account for its findings. It does not hold constant the value of any extraneous explanatory variable. It does not eliminate, and it cannot measure, the influence of such variables upon its findings. It is difficult to justify generalizing its findings to other subjects.

Campbell and Stanley's influential depiction of such studies is worth quoting:

> Basic to scientific evidence . . . is the process of comparison, of recording differences, or of contrast. Any appearance of absolute knowledge, or of intrinsic knowledge about singular isolated objects, is found to be illusory upon analysis. Securing scientific evidence involves making at least one comparison. For such a comparison to be useful, both sides of the comparison should be made with similar care and precision.

In the [one-shot case study], a carefully studied single instance is implicitly compared with other events casually observed and remembered. The inferences are based upon general expectations of what the data would have been had the X not occurred, etc. Such studies often involve tedious collection of specific detail, careful observation, testing, and the like, and in such instances involve the error of *misplaced precision*. How much more valuable the study would be if the one set of observations were reduced by half and the saved effort directed to the study in equal detail of an appropriate comparison instance . . . "Standardized" tests in such case studies provide only very limited help, since the rival sources of difference other than X are so numerous as to render the "standard" reference group almost useless as a "control group." On the same grounds, the many uncontrolled sources of difference between a present case study and potential future ones which might be compared with it are so numerous as to make justification in terms of providing a bench mark for future studies also hopeless. In general, it would be better to apportion the descriptive effort between both sides of an interesting comparison. [Pp. 6–7]

However, the study of a single subject (whether the subject is, for example, a single person, a therapy dyad, or a group) can include careful comparisons of the subject under different conditions, treatments, or levels of a treatment, while at the same time, since only one subject is involved, holding constant those properties of subjects which in group-comparison studies (because in those studies these properties vary from subject to subject) are potential sources of systematic or unsystematic influence upon the outcome of such studies.

Psychoanalysts, disregarding such possibilities for single subject research, tend to identify the single case study with narrative case histories and accounts of treatment. However valuable these are, as vehicles enabling clinicians to share their work with each other, to maintain and enhance skills, to illustrate how a technique is to be carried out or a concept applied, or to generate new hypotheses, they cannot satisfy, *in the form they are usually written*, the canons of eliminative inductivism in order to justify provisional acceptance of a hypothesis as scientifically credible. (However, there are exceptions, as we shall see when later in this book we examine Glymour's explication of Freud's Rat Man case.)

Psychoanalysts like many others tend mistakenly to assume that single case studies are necessarily carried out in the context of discov-

ery rather than the context of justification, that such studies are necessarily nonexperimental rather than experimental, and that nonexperimental studies are incapable of testing causal hypotheses. They do not
appreciate the variety of forms single subject research can take, and how
much more suitable to the context of justification some of these forms
are than others. In this connection, I invite the reader to compare Bolgar's traditional but useful discussion (1965) of the case study method
with Duke's review (1965) of the vast array of problems that even
by then had been confronted in $N = 1$ studies, and to examine the collection of experimental, quasi-experimental, and nonexperimental-
quantitative studies of single subjects provided by Davidson and Costello (1969).

## 1. The Present Status of Single Case Study in Psychoanalysis

In what is now a well-known single case study ("The Two Analyses
of Mr. Z"), a psychoanalyst argues that his comparison of the results of
a first and second analysis, both conducted by himself, of the same
analysand, supports his claim that one kind of psychoanalytic intervention is more effective than another (Kohut, 1979). This psychoanalyst
recognizes, as not every author of a psychoanalytic case study does,
that a comparison (here, between the outcome of one kind of intervention and the outcome of the other) is necessary to make his argument.
There is no sign, however, he knows what is required to make convincing the argument that evidence he presents is related probatively to his
hypothesis (that is, tests the hypothesis). He fails, for example, to es-
tablish unequivocally either that the intended change in intervention was
actually implemented or that there was an actual difference in outcome.

Moreover, he does not even consider, much less eliminate as explanatory candidates, alternative plausible hypotheses that, given our background knowledge without benefit of his hypothesis, might be held to
account for the difference in outcome he claims to have observed. The
psychoanalyst had grown in experience from one analysis to another.
Might not this increase in experience have brought about a different result in the second analysis, whether or not he had made use of the specified new kind of intervention? Might not the first psychoanalysis, as
well as the analysand's maturation and events or altered circumstances
in the period from the first to the second analysis (for example, the
analysand's mother's increasingly evident psychopathology), have led
to changes in the analysand, in what he presented for analysis, or in

how he responded to the psychoanalyst's interventions? Such changes might have brought about the apparent difference in result, even if the specified alteration in intervention had had no effect at all.

At least, there is some attempt in this study to go beyond the vacuous enumerative inductivism so rampant in the psychoanalytic literature. It is generally believed in this literature that phenomena shown to be predictable from the propositions of a theory *necessarily* provide support for those propositions (in the absence of negative instances). That is, these predictable instances or deducible observation statements, if they occur or are true, are supposed to confer scientific credibility upon the theoretical propositions (warrant provisional acceptance of them as true, or make them more likely true than false).[1] At its worst, this enumerative inductivism degenerates into the belief that a mere conjunction of anecdotes (illustrative examples or vignettes) and theoretical propositions somehow confers supportive evidential status on the former with respect to the latter. I am not referring here, of course, to the use of examples to *illustrate*, for purposes of clarification, a concept, or a technique or method. However, that such is the purpose of these examples is rarely made explicit in this literature, often leaving a vague impression that they are offered as evidence for some hypothesis or other.

The psychoanalytic community on the whole continues to take the stand articulated by Hartmann (1959); his words can be and have been (but need not necessarily be) interpreted to favor enumerative inductivism.

> As to the data, it is hard to give, outside the analytic process itself, an impression of the wealth of observational data collected in even one single "case." One frequently refers to the comparatively small number of cases studied in analysis and tends to forget the very great number of actual observations on which we base, in every individual case, the interpretations of an aspect of a patient's character, symptoms and so on. [P. 21]

Hartmann adds the footnote: "Thus every single 'case' represents, for research, hundreds of data of observed regularities, and in hundreds of respects."

Here, we should recall Rapaport's reservations about these data, previously cited in Part One, pp. 2–3.

Even the single case study as typically conceived in psychoanalysis,

1. This belief has already been discredited (in Part One of this book).

in the context of discovery, would be improved by regular inclusion of a precise statement of the hypothesis generated, an account of the observations and theoretical notions that lend the hypothesis some plausibility (not the same as an argument that the hypothesis is scientifically credible because evidence favors it over some other rival hypothesis), and some proposal outlining the circumstances in which or the means by which such a hypothesis might be tested (that is, might achieve scientific credibility). In this latter proposal, of course, the clinical investigator commits himself to a statement of the observations that he would accept as falsifying his hypothesis.

## 2. Conceptual and Methodological Developments in Single Subject Research

A convincing, detailed argument for favoring single subject studies or an "intensive design" over large-$N$ studies or an "extensive design" in clinical research has been given by Chassan (1970, 1979). The argument is repeated for experimental psychology by Robinson and Foster (1979), for educational program research by Kratochwill (1978), and for clinical psychology and psychotherapy research by Kazdin (1980a, 1982) and Leitenberg (1973).

In a group-comparison study, the number of subjects is as large as necessary to demonstrate that the desired effect is not a chance result of sampling. Such a study is an advance over the study of one sample or group, in which, for example, a "percentage of success" is the outcome. This first kind of study has the power, as the second does not, to exclude alternative plausible hypotheses that attribute the obtained outcome to such factors as chance, the natural course of the illness, or placebo. However, group-comparison studies as carried out are often riddled with what are—given the stakes for knowledge and practice—breathtakingly nontrivial defects, which given the realities of clinical research are largely unavoidable.

It is not easy to obtain truly random samples in clinical practice and settings. But then the effects of extraneous variables cannot be assumed to be randomized and equivalent in the compared groups, and these groups cannot be assumed to be similar with respect to all relevant variables other than the explanatory variable(s). Nor can these nonrandom samples be assumed to be representative of the populations from which they are presumably drawn. Therefore, the investigator lacks justification to generalize his findings to these populations. (Even if the samples were random, that does not guarantee they are representative; a non-representative sample may be selected, although presumably rarely, by chance.)

Further, when experimental interventions are involved, subjects may not be randomly allocated to the treatments being compared. (The selection process may make samples systematically different, in ways other than the fact that the members of the samples have been exposed to different treatments.) Therefore, alternative plausible hypotheses that attribute the study's outcome to the effects of the selection-for-treatment process itself cannot easily be excluded.

The absence of random sampling and random allocation raises questions about what Stanley and Campbell call the internal validity of such studies. How is the investigator to evaluate the hypothesis that his outcome is due to chance and not to his explanatory variable(s) if he has not made use of random sampling and random allocation? How can he argue that, if the study were repeated with other samples, that these samples would differ in their properties by chance alone, and that, if that were their only difference, then an outcome supporting his hypothesis over the hypothesis attributing the outcome solely to chance would in each repetition of the study be the same?

The absence of random sampling also raises questions about what Campbell and Stanley call the external validity of such studies. If the sample is not representative, to what domain can the findings be generalized?

More important, the comparison of groups in terms of the mean or average effect of different factors, conditions, or treatments—which is the very heart of the group-comparison method—tends to obscure the nature of these effects. An average outcome is no single individual's outcome. Some members of each group may have responded in differing degrees in one direction, others in differing degrees in the opposite direction, although the groups differ (if they do differ) *on the average* in one direction only. The question "Upon exactly what members of the domain, with what characteristics, does a treatment have a particular effect?" is not answered by such a study, since it does not identify which members of the group were affected. Generalization from such a study to a particular individual patient in clinical practice is, therefore, not possible. For the same reason, implications for theory are not clear.

This problem is likely to be exacerbated when, as is often the case, the definition of the category (diagnosis) to which those subjected to different conditions or treatments are assigned, as well as the definitions of the different conditions or treatments, and of the possible effects of these different conditions or treatments, are vague, global, fuzzy, or otherwise ill-conceived. Samples of subjects supposedly belonging to the same category are in fact in most respects extremely heterogenous. It is difficult, then, to know what has had what effect, if any, upon what kind of subject, and to what population conclusions may be generalized.

It is also difficult to demonstrate that a difference between groups is due to the explanatory variable, even when different conditions or treatments do indeed have different effects. The differences in effect must be so great that they can "stand out" over and above the background noise of differences among subjects in each group. That is, differences between groups must be so great they cannot be easily explained as another expression of the differences among subjects. Otherwise, the alternative hypothesis that differences (in fact resulting from the conditions or treatments) are simply a chance expression of how individual differences among subjects have fallen cannot be rejected.

It is not only that true differences in the effects of different conditions or treatments are difficult to demonstrate. Insignificant or idiosyncratic differences can be given too great importance. One or two members of a group may swing a group so far one way, despite the positions of the other members, that a group which would not otherwise be judged to differ in any significant way from another group is judged to do so.

Further, as the groups become large, almost any difference between them becomes "statistically significant." That is, it becomes extremely unlikely, though possible, that the difference, given the large numbers involved, is due to a chance process alone. The difference in effect is statistically significant, even if such a difference is so small as to lack all practical or theoretical significance.

With regard to psychotherapy research in particular, the recent report of the American Psychiatric Association's Commission on Psychotherapies (Karasu et al., 1982), as well as Kazdin's recent discussion of research design (1980a), make clear that the problem of satisfying the canons of eliminative inductivism is not just a problem for psychoanalysis but is a problem for any kind of psychotherapy research. These works, it seems to me, especially in their consideration of the difficulties in obtaining and holding on to different kinds of control groups, imply that many of the difficulties in solving this problem are inherent in any attempt to satisfy these canons solely by the group-comparison method, a method which unfortunately is held up by Grünbaum among others as *the* way to satisfy these canons.

Notwithstanding the defects of the group-comparison method, it may be, of course, necessary to use it in order to answer a policy question about the overall effect on an entire population of one condition or treatment compared to one or more other conditions or treatments. Interest here is in the aggregate, not the individual. The question to be answered is the following. Whatever the effect on any particular individual, does the average difference between groups—for example, an overall improvement in outcome of treatment—which is to be expected on the basis of such a study justify introducing a change in condition or treatment for the population as a whole?

Intensive study of a single case, with the single case itself regarded as a domain, changes the problem from random sampling of subjects to random sampling of occasions (time-slices of the subject) or of materials to which the subject responds or with which the subject interacts; and from random allocation of subjects to treatments, conditions, or levels of treatment to random allocation of treatments, conditions, or levels of treatment to occasions (time-slices of the subject). Edgington (1972, 1980a, 1980b, 1980c) focuses especially on the use of randomization in experimental single subject research.

The problem of the internal validity of a study can in part be dealt with by the direct replication of that study with the same (or same kind of) subject. The problem of external validity or generalizability to populations becomes a problem of generalizing to other time-slices of the subject; or, if generalization to other subjects is sought, a matter of systematic replication of the single subject study. In systematic replication, the study is repeated with other subjects, or in other settings. With each replication, the subject or setting is the same with the exception of one property or feature; properties of the subject or setting are considered then to be systematically varied. The investigator may thus determine the scope of his hypothesis—the range of kinds of subjects or settings over which it holds.

The use of direct and systematic replication in single subject research bears some resemblance to the use of "combinatory techniques" in assessing the efficacy of therapy. Different studies of different treatments may be scored as showing positive, negative, or no significant effects of a treatment; the scores obtained for different treatments are compared (the "box score method"). However, this method tends to give equal weight to poor studies (which preponderate) and good studies, ignores differences in the size of the groups in different studies, has no way of evaluating by how much one kind of treatment differs from another, and in general possesses no rational basis for combining studies. A statistical "meta-analysis" of the outcomes of a large number of studies may permit a conclusion that is not justified by any single study, by taking into account in the meta-analysis the size of the effect reported in each study. However, criteria for inclusion of studies to be combined tend to be arbitrary, and generalizations are limited by the very different kinds and the nonrepresentativeness of the patients, therapists, and treatments in the individual studies combined (Karasu et al., 1982, pp. 115–126). The problems with combinatory techniques are not in general characteristically problems of single subject research or of the direct or systematic replication of single subject studies.

Sidman (1960) provides a conceptual foundation for the treatment of internal and external validity in experimental single subject research. Sidman's ideas about the use of systematic replication to support claims of generalizability in experimental single subject research are, I believe, applicable to nonexperimental single subject research as well.

The psychoanalyst must be particularly cautious with respect to such works as Sidman's. He is likely to reject them out-of-hand, because the research interests and questions, the variables mentioned, and the terminology may be in an alien conceptual framework (for example, that of Skinner, who himself argued for the detailed study of functional relationships in single organisms). However, the methodological issues, research designs, and modes of reasoning presented in these works can and should be abstracted from the particular content of the research examples. Hersen and Barlow (1976), who make extensive use of Sidman's foundation, themselves point out that Breuer and Freud's case of Anna O. is an example of what in their framework is called the "multiple baseline design." It is the nature of the argument about the relation between hypothesis and evidence that matters here, not parochial theoretical commitments.

Hersen and Barlow (1976), in their discussion of experimental studies of therapeutic change in single subjects, make use of designs suggested by Campbell and Stanley (1963). Campbell and Stanley, in a consideration of research on teaching, present ways to study single subjects (a classroom, a school) quasi-experimentally, that is, ways involving some control over when an intervention occurs, but not involving random selection of subjects. Their time-series design calls for obtaining multiple observations of a single subject (which could be a person as well as a group) over time before an intervention occurs, in order to obtain a baseline with which to compare the multiple observations of that subject which are obtained over time following the intervention. (Gottman, 1973, has been responsible for developing ways to analyze data obtained in studies using a time-series design.) Campbell and Stanley's equivalent time-samples design involves multiple alternations of the baseline condition and treatment condition which are to be compared. Their equivalent materials design involves alternation over time of the kind of materials or entities to which the subject responds or with which the subject interacts. Each of these designs makes it possible to exclude alternative hypotheses which might otherwise account for the outcome of a study, and the influence of variables which might otherwise limit the generalizability of that study.

Single subject research has another major advantage over group-comparison research. It is possible in single subject research to enhance the validity and reliability of measurement of variables of interest by individualizing instruments for obtaining data. Instead of employing a scattershot approach, which in a necessarily general way touches upon or requires measurements of a variety of possible kinds of behaviors or manifestations of states, each of which may be relevant or applicable to some members of a group and not to others, single subject research can focus upon just those kinds of manifestations or behaviors which the investigator has reason to believe are especially significant in or relevant to the particular subject he studies. For example, statements included in a set of statements to be used by the subject to describe various aspects of himself, or other social or cultural entities important to him, can be drawn from a population of statements the subject has actually made (Edelson and Jones, 1954). The development and use of Q-methodology by Stephenson (1953, 1974) and the development and use of the Personal Questionnaire by Shapiro (1961, 1963, 1966) exemplify this potential advantage of single subject research.

Furthermore, an investigator may use Q-methodology, the Personal Questionnaire, or Osgood's Semantic Differential (Osgood et al., 1957), for example, to study, and test hypotheses about, subjective phenomena. So, responding and ordering a set of statements in Q-methodology, the subject can represent his ego-ideal, an object-representation, or his self-representation (all of interest to the psychoanalyst) in a way that permits quantitative operations and, therefore, precise comparisons. In single subject research, methodological innovation need not sacrifice either the internal (subjective) frame of reference or the requirement for explicit, repeatable, objective observations (measurements).

Different observations on the same subject in single subject research cannot be regarded as independent in the same sense that observations in group-comparison research are designed to be independent. In group-comparison research, if different subjects are selected randomly, that justifies the assumption they do not influence each other. This question about independence poses a problem for single subject research. Are statistical reasoning and statistical tests of hypotheses in single subject research justifiable, when such reasoning and tests, for the most part, involve the assumption that observations or measurements are independent?

There are a variety of answers to this question proposed in the literature (Edgington, 1967, 1980a; Kazdin, 1976, 1980b, 1981; Kratochwill, 1978). One may try to justify the use of the usual statistical methods; develop new statistical methods to deal with the kinds of dependencies which violate the independence assumption; or, eschewing statistical reasoning and methods, seek to achieve effects that are clearly clinically or theoretically significant, such large effects indeed that it can be argued that an effect of such magnitude, obtained in direct relation to the presence of an intervention, excludes as implausible the alternative hypothesis that this effect is due to chance or random fluctuations produced by extraneous variables.

In an approach that is especially apposite to single subject research in psychoanalysis, Herbst (1970) views the single subject as a "world" to be investigated, that is, as an independent domain. He raises the possibility that a set of variables may have some relation in many such domains (subjects), but suggests that each domain must be studied separately. For, though some relation between members of a set of variables may exist in more than one domain, that relation can change in various ways—in the value of specific constants or parameters, or in the form or strength of the relation—from subject to subject (domain to domain). If this is so, laws tested in single subject research will specify that variables have a relation in each domain (subject), but that constants or parameters, or the form or strength of the relation, may vary from domain to domain. Indeed, what causes these changes in the laws themselves from domain to domain is an important problem for single subject research (Rozeboom, 1961).[2]

2. A more detailed discussion of the literature on single subject research, and the topics I have touched upon here, as well as of the implications for psychoanalysis of these developments, will be found in my forthcoming book *Single Subject Research*.

### 3. Single Subject Research: Implications for Psychoanalysis

The single subject may be but is not necessarily a single person (for example, a patient). The single subject might just as well be: a single dyad (for example, a married couple, a psychotherapist-and-patient dyad), a single family, a single small group, or a single organization (hospital, hospital unit, or therapeutic community).

Intensive studies of single cases may be used, contrary to a widely held misconception, to test as well as to generate hypotheses. In fact, single subject research may legitimately have any one of a variety of objectives. The psychoanalytic literature in particular often fails to make explicit which objective a particular study is designed to achieve, or confuses one objective with another. Blurring distinctions between objectives can lead to the false impression that achieving one objective (illustrating a method or concept) entails achievement of another (providing evidential support for an empirical claim). Consistently making explicit in this literature which objective any particular single case study has would in itself enhance the scientific status of psychoanalysis.

1. *Theoretical single case studies*, in the context of discovery, may achieve any one or number of the following objectives. A theoretical single case study may:

*a*) pick out facts of interest as not yet explained or at least not yet satisfactorily explained, but calling for explanation;

*b*) make clear what background knowledge, what pretheoretic knowledge, or what knowledge of some theory other than the theory at issue, is presupposed in observing and describing these facts;

*c*) define a theoretic concept, and clarify it by illustrating its defining features as exemplified in the single case, or by showing how it might be applied in a single case;

*d*) generate theoretic and nontheoretic hypotheses, which make empirically testable truth claims about a domain; or

*e*) show that a set of interrelated but independent nontheoretic and/or theoretic statements is logically consistent (no one statement is a logical contradiction of any other, even though not every statement is necessarily true of every subject), by showing that all are simultaneously true of at least one particular subject.

Using a single case study to generate a hypothesis (objective *d*) involves showing what an investigator "means" or has in mind in formulating a hypothesis. To this end, an investigator may describe the phenomena that are the apparent occasion for his invention of a stated hypothesis. These are also the kind of phenomena his hypothesis is intended to explain. Using observations in this way should be sharply distinguished, as it often is not in the psychoanalytic literature, from concluding that such observations are probative evidence, which justify provisional acceptance of a hypothesis as true. Such a conclusion should in fact be explicitly disclaimed, lest it be taken for granted in subsequent writings by others.

2. *Empirical single case studies*, in the context of justification, may achieve any one or number of the following objectives. An empirical single case study may:

*a*) offer a method to improve the reliability or validity with which a variable of interest is measured;[3]

*b*) present a set of measurements of a variable of interest and suggest how to account for observed changes in this variable;

*c*) test a hypothesis, by obtaining evidence that is actually probative because it has been obtained in such a way that the investigator can argue that it justifies provisionally accepting a hypothesis as true over one or more rival or alternative hypotheses;

*d*) refine a hypothesis with respect to its scope, by systematically replicating a single case study, for example, and arguing that the conclusions derived from the study of a single subject are or are not generalizable to other subjects;

*e*) seize the opportunity to describe in as much detail as possible a rare or difficult-to-observe case of $X$, even if no hypothesis is generated or tested;[4]

*f*) illustrate a technique or method, or, in other words, show how something is done.[5]

3. "Measurement" includes: assigning entities in a domain to one member of an exhaustive set of mutually exclusive classes or categories, rank ordering entities in a domain as "more than" or "less than" on some dimension, assigning an amount (a number of equal units of some quantity) to entities in a domain. The first two kinds of measurement are more applicable in psychoanalytic case studies than many psychoanalysts have realized. (The entities in single subject research, of course, will not be different subjects. I discuss this further in Chapter 6.)

I have already mentioned the advantage single subject research has in being able to individualize measuring instruments in order to increase the reliability and validity of obtained measurements.

4. This may be an overvalued objective. There is no guarantee an investigator, who tries for the sake of the future to describe "everything," will choose to make just those observations that will turn out in the light of later knowledge, or with respect to later questions or hypotheses, to be interesting, relevant, or crucial.

5. This should be distinguished, as it often is not, from providing evidential support

An important distinction needs to be made, with respect to objective
*d* above, between the validity of a single case study (Is the hypothesis
true of this case?) and the generalizability of the conclusion of a single
case study. A single subject may be regarded as a member of a class of
subjects (a member of a domain of subjects), in which case generalization of a valid conclusion about this subject to other subjects in the class
or domain becomes an important problem. Systematic replication is one
way to deal with it. If the study is replicated—using subjects from that
domain who vary in a systematic way on particular dimensions from
one another—and the hypothesis is supported in all such replications,
then it can be argued that the conclusion can be generalized to other
members of the domain.

On the other hand, the single subject may be regarded as a domain of
entities (for example, psychological entities or events). The primary
question may then be: Is this subject a certain kind of domain? For example, do the psychological entities or events satisfy certain laws? The
question of generalizability may become a question of generalizing to
other times, places, or stages of development occupied by, or to other
conditions impinging upon, this subject.

In any event, we always want to know first: Is this hypothesis true of
this particular subject? It may be that that is all we want to know. However, we may also want to know whether the hypothesis true of this subject under these circumstances is true of this subject under other circumstances, or is true of other subjects as well. Questions of validity and
questions of generalizability are argued differently.

An empirical single case study may also argue, for example, about
the generalizability (not necessarily the validity) of findings by:

*a*) describing a single subject that constitutes a counterexample, in
order to cast doubt upon, to falsify, or to limit the scope of a universal
generalization;

*b*) describing a representative case—a case which is a case of *X* if
anything is a case of *X*—in order to argue that what is true of, or what is
a propensity of given strength belonging to, this representative case will
be true of, or will be a propensity of some strength belonging to, other
cases of *X*, just to the extent these other cases are cases of *X*.[6]

Certain misconceptions about single subject research should there-

---

for claims about the effectiveness of a technique or method (an example of objective
*c* above).

6. See, for example, Shontz (1965).

fore be abandoned by psychoanalysts. That an investigator does single subject research does not necessarily imply, as the cited literature demonstrates, that he has an exclusive interest in, or is limited to, either:

   *a*) studying what is unique to one, or what is common to many;

   *b*) studying an intrapersonal domain, or a domain of persons;

   *c*) studying a subjective or an objective aspect of nature;

   *d*) doing basic or applied research;

   *e*) generating hypotheses in the context of discovery, or testing hypotheses in the context of justification;

   *f*) formulating deterministic or probabilistic hypotheses;

   *g*) formulating narratives, which do not specify analytically distinguished variables, or explicitly defining and using variables, which may be measured on nominal, ordinal, interval, or ratio scales;

   *h*) describing or inferring;

   *i*) proceeding deductively or inductively in testing hypotheses;

   *j*) using or not using statistical methods or reasoning;

   *k*) making the same kind of observation(s) repeatedly over a sequence of occasions (longitudinal investigation), or making different kinds of observations on one occasion (cross-sectional investigation);

   *l*) obtaining evidence nonexperimentally or experimentally.[7]

7. Support for, and examples bearing upon, these assertions about single subject research will be found also in my forthcoming book, previously mentioned.

# 5     The Objective-Propensity Interpretation of Probability in Single Subject Research

If psychoanalysis wants to respond effectively to the challenge of eliminative inductivism, while it does not need to rely solely on, it cannot afford entirely to eschew (either in its formulation of hypotheses or in its study of single cases), such powerful conceptual tools as are provided by the theory of probability and by statistical reasoning about the relation between hypothesis and evidence. Chassan (1953, 1956, 1960, 1961, 1962), in particular, has repeatedly argued this point, although as far as I can tell his papers have gone largely (although not entirely) unnoticed by psychoanalysts.[1]

## 1. Probability

The calculus of probability enables the investigator to calculate, given the probabilities of certain events or outcomes, the probabilities of other events or outcomes (Kyburg, 1970). As a purely formal calculus, the theory of probability is and can be interpreted in a variety of ways (Nagel, 1939; Salmon, 1966, 1970; Skyrms, 1975; Suppes, 1970).

The probability of an event or outcome can be interpreted, for examples, as:

1. a measure of the subjective degree of belief that the event or outcome will occur;

2. the relative frequency of the event or outcome in a population or collective, or the limiting relative frequency of the event or outcome in a long-run sequence of events or outcomes.

A major problem with the first interpretation is that it is difficult to justify a priori assignments of subjective degrees of belief to certain events or outcomes. But these are needed in order to calculate from them the subjective degree of belief that some other event or outcome will occur.

A major problem with the second interpretation is that it is difficult to

---

1. S. Lustman, when he taught about the research uses of psychoanalysis, referred to Chassan's work.

justify assigning a probability to a single outcome, or to an occurrence on one occasion of a particular event, from knowledge of the relative frequency of that event or outcome in a population or collective, or from knowledge of the limiting relative frequency of that event or outcome in a long-run sequence of events or outcomes. The first probability is a property of an individual or "single case"; the second probability is the property of a collective or population of individuals or cases. The reasoning by which one converts a property of the collective into a property of an individual tends to seem somewhat arbitrary (as I think it is in Popper, 1959a, pp. 209–212).

A new interpretation of probability has been proposed (Giere, 1973, 1979a, 1980; Hacking, 1965; Mellor, 1971; Popper, 1959a, 1959b; Railton, 1978). The probability of an event or outcome is best interpreted as a measure of the strength of an objective disposition or propensity. This disposition or propensity is a property "in Nature" of some individual, some arrangement in Nature, or some set-up (for example, an experimental set-up) or device, like the device which tosses coins, where the outcome of each toss is independent of every other, or which selects members of a population at random, where the outcome of each selection is independent of every other. The disposition is the propensity of a set-up, arrangement, device, or individual to produce the outcome or event under certain conditions (that is, when a certain kind of trial is conducted on that set-up, device, or individual). A trial is conducted, for example, when a coin is tossed, a member of a population is selected at random, an individual is observed or measured on a chosen occasion, a car traverses a particular route, or an organism is conceived.

This interpretation seems especially suitable, when interest is in data of single subject research. In the propensity interpretation of probability, the relative frequency of an event or outcome in a population, collective, or long-run sequence is simply evidence for the hypothesized strength of the disposition or propensity of a set-up, arrangement, device, or individual to produce that event or outcome. The relative frequency of some action or state of a single subject under specified conditions is simply evidence for the strength of a hypothetical disposition or propensity of that subject to display the behavior or the state under those conditions. Such a disposition or propensity is an objective property of the single subject, a property that conceivably could change under other conditions or over time.

This formulation conceives of a single subject as a nondeterministic (a probabilistic or stochastic) system—and suggests both that many, if not most or all, explanatory hypotheses of psychoanalysis can and should be formulated as nondeterministic hypotheses, and that the calculus of probability and statistical reasoning can and should play a role in testing such hypotheses.

## 2. Statistical Methods and Reasoning

Interest in nonparametric statistics has been growing for some time (Edgington, 1980c; Feinstein, 1977; Freeman, 1965; Hays, 1973; Leach, 1979; Siegel, 1956; Watson and McGaw, 1980). These statistical methods are appropriate for use in analyzing classificatory or ordinal data (measurements on classificatory or ordinal scales). These are the kind of data that are especially likely to be obtained in single subject and most clinical research. Such methods also avoid some assumptions about data (made in using parametric statistics) which are so unlikely in most clinical studies their presence undermines the cogency of arguments about the relation between hypothesis and evidence in such studies.

More recently, especially with the availability of computers, exact probability or randomization tests (which are nonparametric) have become increasingly practical to use (Edgington, 1980c). These methods have always been attractive, both because of the clarity of the reasoning involved and the rudimentary arithmetic required. Such features are important for any attempt to encourage the use or at least appreciation of statistical reasoning and methods by psychoanalysts and other clinicians, who often seem to be both number-phobic and innocent of knowledge of statistical reasoning. The sophisticated development of statistical reasoning is one of the glories of contemporary science, and deserves more attention from the psychoanalytic research community.

# 6 A Strategy Based Upon the Nonstatement View of Theory for Formulating the Theory of Psychoanalysis

In this chapter, in the interest of making explicit what agreement and disagreement there might be among those who argue about testing psychoanalytic hypotheses as to just what these hypotheses are, I shall briefly summarize what I consider to be major theoretical ideas in psychoanalysis. I shall go on to outline a strategy for formulating these ideas systematically and rigorously as the core of psychoanalytic theory, and then explicate the nonstatement view of theory which suggests this particular strategy.

Next, I shall consider in some detail in terms of the nonstatement view of theory just what kind of domains are of interest to psychoanalysis. The question of the kind of domains that are of interest to psychoanalysis encompasses the following questions, which are addressed by me here. What kinds of entities does psychoanalysis study? What are the nontheoretic concepts used by psychoanalysis to pick out those properties of and relations between or among entities that constitute the facts psychoanalysis seeks to explain? What are the theoretic concepts used by psychoanalysis to pick out those properties and relations that enter into explanations of these facts? What domain among all others is first and foremost intended as that domain to which psychoanalytic theory will be successfully applied, if there is any domain at all to which it can be successfully applied?

In conclusion, I shall attempt a tentative sketch of the way psychoanalytic theory might start to look if one were to attempt a formulation of it in terms of the nonstatement view of theory.

Let me say at once, and most emphatically, that this sketch is designed only to be heuristic. I want mainly to present it to convince my readers that adopting the strategy for formulating psychoanalytic theory suggested earlier on in the chapter may have a useful, even exciting, outcome, with implications for research in psychoanalysis. I do not, however, intend to claim or imply that the theory of psychoanalysis has at this time already reached the point where a precise, rigorous, and even quasi-formal, much less formal, statement of it is possible. So, for example, when I speak in this sketch of psychoanalytic "laws," I certainly do not intend to claim or imply that we are now in a position even to identify such laws, much less to state them precisely and rigorously.

The discussion of psychoanalytic theory in Chapters 6 and 7 is essential to appreciate what kind of hypotheses I have in mind when, in Part Three, I reject the claim that psychoanalytic hypotheses cannot be tested in the psychoanalytic situation, and to understand fully various details of my response to that claim. However, this discussion of the theory is preparatory, relatively lengthy (though, even at that, necessarily condensed), somewhat fragmentary (as a beginning is), and perhaps controversial. It may, therefore, here and now, merely serve to distract some readers on a first reading of the book from the main line of my argument.

So, I can easily imagine that a reader, having Grünbaum's position now freshly in mind, might grow impatient with Chapters 6 and 7 and, wanting to get on with the argument, prefer on a first reading to skip them. Since these chapters, addressing as they do the question of the nature of psychoanalytic theory in the light of a novel conception of theory, may well benefit in any event from a later, rather slow, careful reading, I suggest that the reader who wants to maintain the momentum of the argument do so, if he wishes, by proceeding directly to Part Three. He can do so without too much loss of continuity, although for a grasp at the least of such terms and phrases as "domain" and ". . . is a Freudian system," he will need to return to Chapter 6.

## 1. Major Theoretical Ideas in Psychoanalysis

In accounting for my selection of the major theoretical ideas in psychoanalysis, I should make it clear at once that I do not regard metapsychology in psychoanalysis as a collection of the most abstract, general substantive propositions of psychoanalysis (as opposed to its close-to-experience or less general propositions). Nor do I regard it as a general theory of the mind (as opposed to a "clinical theory," which presumably might be limited to explaining clinical—that is, psychopathological—phenomena).

First, I do not regard most of what goes under the name "metapsychology" as a theory, which makes substantive claims about the world. (A substantive claim, for example, is made by the universal generalization "There is no neurosis without sexual disorder." This kind of statement is not characteristic of metapsychology.) Second, I do not believe that it is wise for any theory to adopt as its domain so unlimited and ill-defined a realm as is implied by the use of the phrase "a general theory of the mind." (For further discussion of these and similar points, see the discussions of the status of metapsychology in Edelson, 1977, pp. 1–11, and 1978, pp. 129–134.)

As I read metapsychology, it appears to me to be, rather than a set of propositions about the world, a set of proposals for building theory. These proposals prescribe primarily which theoretical concepts should be chosen to specify just those properties and relations of entities in the domain of interest to psychoanalysis that are essential to explain the facts psychoanalytic theory is committed to explain.

If metapsychology is so regarded, then one may find it useful to refer to metapsychological writings in an attempt to identify a core set of theoretical ideas in psychoanalysis. Anyone who makes this attempt or who wrestles with the questions addressed in this chapter should be familiar at least not only with the works of Freud but as well with the notable efforts to systematize psychoanalytic theory of Arlow and Brenner (1964), Fenichel (1945), Gill (1963), Klein (1976), Rapaport (1950, 1951, 1953, 1959a, 1959b, 1960), Rubinstein (1967, 1974, 1975, 1976), Schur (1966), and Waelder (1960). Waelder's book, the work of someone who knew science, is unjustly neglected.

The following ideas comprise a core set of theoretical ideas in psychoanalysis. (It will, I think, be clear to the reader that they are not completely congruent with those upon which Grünbaum focuses having to do with the efficacy of therapy and etiology of neuroses.) Other ideas, of course, must be added to these, as psychoanalysis extends the range of facts it attempts to explain. However, I do not believe that any attempt to formulate psychoanalytic theory more rigorously than it now is formulated can fail to deal with this core set of ideas.

*a) Why and how is a senseless mental content produced?* A mental content calls for explanation if it does not make sense. "Does not make sense" has two meanings here. One, the mental content is purposeless. That is, the person who produces it is not aware of any sequence of mental contents leading to a desired goal to which this mental content belongs. Two, the mental content is experienced by the person as a failure of some sort, a sign of a difficulty in achieving or expressing something, but one which is inexplicable in "ordinary" terms. That is, no physical lesion or physiological dysfunction, no environmental intrusion or deficiency, adequately accounts for the failure, difficulty, or incapacity. No appeal to physical or environmental causes can be demonstrated to be sufficient to explain the senselessness of the mental content. The theoretical terms of psychoanalysis are not needed to recognize or identify a mental content as senseless.

*b) Mental processes are purposive.* Underlying the adoption of the senseless mental content as the kind of fact to be explained by psychoanalysis is the assumption that mental processes are purposive. If they do not seem to be purposive, that is something to be explained. A psychoanalytic explanation aims to discover what purpose governs the production of an apparently purposeless mental content and (this is essential) to show how that content has come to seem senseless. Such an explanation will identify at least one goal-oriented sequence of mental contents to which the senseless mental content does belong. A senseless mental content makes sense once the person who produced it recognizes, feels, acknowledges that it belongs to such a sequence—and perhaps also how it has come to be disconnected from that sequence, how it has come to seem senseless in the first place.

*c) There can be no senseless mental content (which is unrelated to any conscious purpose) without unconscious purposes.* Some or all of the goal-oriented sequence(s) to which a senseless mental content actually belongs are unconscious—that is, relatively inaccessible to consciousness. In some cases, what is unconscious is that conscious but not related mental contents (including senseless mental contents) are in fact connected—that is, are related to each other by virtue of belonging to the same goal-oriented sequence.

In general, any weakening of commitment to or lessening of resources for, or any suspending of the execution of, conscious purposive sequences will result in an increasing dominance over mental life of unconscious purposes.

*d) The relation of senseless mental contents to unconscious purposes is governed by primary process.* Senseless mental contents belong to goal-oriented sequences either directly or indirectly. A senseless mental content may belong directly to a goal-oriented sequence, but in that case it has been disconnected from that sequence. A senseless mental content may belong indirectly to a goal-oriented sequence by virtue of its connections or allusions to mental contents directly belonging to the sequence.

Conscious mental contents—that is, mental contents in consciousness or having relatively easy access to consciousness—allude to, stand for, or are signs of unconscious mental contents by virtue of certain relations with them. These relations are quite different from those among conscious mental contents that are permitted in or required for veridical perception or logical thought, or for the accurate representation of such thought or perception using symbolic media. The former kind of relations are encompassed by the term "primary process," the latter by the term "secondary process."

Condensations must be unpacked, displacements reversed, symbols translated, isolations abolished, and uses of imagery (and action?) to allude to or stand for thoughts must be understood, in order to show that the senseless mental content belongs directly or indirectly to a goal-sequence (Fenichel, 1941, pp. 42–43).

*e) At least one unconscious purpose to which a senseless mental content is related has as its end or goal the expression or gratification of sexual or hostile impulses or wishes.* These impulses or wishes are peremptory. That is, these sequence although unconscious persist in force, are in the status of being run off or executed (see Miller et al., 1960), and tend to preempt resources required for the execution of other sequences. Their peremptoriness intensifies periodically, sometimes in response to external opportunities, inducements, or temptations, but essentially irrespective of whether these exist or not. These sequences are consummatory. That is, gratification occurs if the sequence reaches its termination—the actual performance of a particular kind of act with a particular kind of object, which is followed by a decrease in the peremptoriness or intensity of the wish or impulse.

A conscious mental content that alludes to, stands for, or is a sign of an unconscious mental content belonging to a sequence leading to gratification (or fulfillment) of a sexual or hostile impulse or wish is called a derivative of that impulse or wish.

*f ) Such sexual or hostile impulses or wishes have their origin in infantile life, where they are represented in psychic life by fantasies, which have since become relatively inaccessible to consciousness.* An impulse or wish is a tendency to repeat the execution of a sequence which has previously reached gratification. The origin of sexual impulses or wishes is ultimately innate, although influenced or modified by experience. These impulses or wishes have preset phases of development, marked by changes in object and mode of gratification. Are hostile impulses or wishes innate, or do such impulses or wishes have their origins instead in experiences of the thwarting of gratification of sexual or other wishes? This question remains unanswered.

*g) If the gratification of a sexual or hostile impulse is thwarted by an obstacle, the goal-oriented sequence terminates in imagining the gratification, that is, in wish-fulfillment.* The prototypical wish-fulfillment is fantasy. Wish-fulfillment may be hallucinatory as in dreams (a product of imagination is believed to be a perception). Wish-fulfillment may also involve (stereotypical) interpretation of ambiguous elements in actual experience, for example, attributing certain motives to oneself and others, or endowing another with one's own characteristics through projection or externalization, or oneself with another's characteristics through introjection or identification, in such a way that it seems a wish or impulse is at least partially (and repeatedly) gratified. Imagining a gratifying state of affairs results in a merely transient, partial decrease in the peremptoriness of the wish or impulse.

   *h) There can be no senseless mental content without unconscious intrapsychic conflict.* A conflict occurs when an attempt to execute a sequence leading to the gratification in actuality (or the fulfillment in fantasy) of sexual or hostile impulses or wishes instigates an attempt to execute a sequence leading to the avoidance of harm.

   A conflict occurs when a person believes that the gratification of a sexual or hostile impulse or wish places him in danger of being harmed. The origin of this belief is in varying degrees both innate (which may mean "invented" as in fantasy, irrespective of, or making use of minimal cues from, external reality) and an outcome of (arises in or is exacerbated by) infantile experiences. Harm includes separation from a valued object, the loss of a valued body part, or the loss of love or self-esteem. The danger of harm is signaled by painful affects—appraisals of actual or imagined states of affairs as involving actual or imagined thwartings of, or threats contingent upon, gratification or fulfillment of impulses or wishes. Such painful affects instigate execution of sequences leading to the avoidance of harm—and eventually the execution of sequences leading to the avoidance of the painful affects themselves.

   Sequences leading to avoidance of harm or danger involve defenses. Defenses are operations upon or transformations of mental contents, including operations denying mental contents access to consciousness. These mental contents belong to sequences leading to gratification (or fulfillment) of sexual or hostile impulses or wishes. Defenses change the properties of mental contents, replace them by other mental contents, or shift them to other sequences. The results of these transformations in turn may be prevented from achieving access to consciousness. Defenses can involve denying access to consciousness of some or all of a sequence that itself includes defensive operations.[1]

   1. Strictly speaking, processes are never accessible to consciousness. Only contents, all of which belong to goal-governed or purposive sequences, achieve access to consciousness or are actively (purposively) prevented from achieving access to consciousness.

In general, given an unconscious conflict, any weakening of commitment to or lessening of resources for, or any suspending of or interference with the execution of, sequences leading to the avoidance of harm or danger, will increase the preemption of such commitments or resources by, and the intensification of the peremptoriness of, sequences leading to the gratification or fulfillment of sexual or hostile impulses.

## 2. A Strategy for Formulating Psychoanalytic Theory

A strategy for achieving, some time in the future, a more rigorous explicit formulation of psychoanalytic theory than we now have might include the following steps.

*a*) Make explicit what kinds of facts are to be explained by psychoanalytic theory. A domain of psychoanalysis is a set of individual entities (e.g., a set of mental contents produced by a single subject) and the properties of and relations between or among these entities. Any domain is a possible domain of psychoanalysis if the individual entities that belong to it can be described by the nontheoretic or pretheoretic terms of psychoanalysis. One may apply such terms (for example, ". . . does not make sense") to individual entities in such a domain without knowledge of psychoanalytic theory, although one may need knowledge of other theories to apply them. Such nontheoretic or pretheoretic terms are used to state the facts psychoanalysis is committed to explain, and so to report basic or fundamental empirical observations in psychoanalysis. It should be clear that a term is nontheoretic only with respect to a particular theory. A nontheoretic term is not "theory-free."

*b*) Make explicit what minimal set of theoretic terms is required by psychoanalytic theory. A possible domain of psychoanalysis (for example, a set of mental contents produced by a single subject) is also a theoretic domain of psychoanalysis if the theoretic terms of psychoanalysis (for example, ". . . is a derivative of . . . ," ". . . is unconscious") describe properties of or relations between or among the entities which belong or which are inferred to belong to the domain.

*c*) Using this set of nontheoretic and theoretic terms, make explicit the fundamental laws or hypotheses that are intended to be true of the actual domains of psychoanalytic theory (for example, "There is no senseless mental content without unconscious intrapsychic conflict"). A theoretic domain of psychoanalysis is also an actual domain of psychoanalysis if it satisfies a specified set of such psychoanalytic laws or hypotheses.

*d*) Define a theoretical predicate such as ". . . is a Freudian system." The definition will have the form "a domain is a Freudian system if and only if *T*," where *T* is the set of psychoanalytic laws or hypotheses which a domain must satisfy in order for the theoretical predicate ". . . is a Freudian system" to be true of it.

*e*) Select at least one domain—for example, a single subject who produces a senseless mental content of a certain kind (dream, parapraxis, neurotic symptom)—of which the theoretical predicate is intended to be true. If the theoretical predicate is true of any domain, it is certainly true of this intended domain.

*f*) Formulate and empirically test a theoretical hypothesis about this intended domain (that it is a Freudian system), and then about additional specified domains of interest (additional subjects). Such theoretical hypotheses will have the form "*A* is a Freudian system," where *A* is a specified domain (for example, "Mr. A is a Freudian system").

*g*) Add special laws or hypotheses to the core set of laws or hypotheses. These special laws will be true of subsets of, but not of all, actual domains (that is, will be true of some subjects and not of others, or of all subjects who produce neurotic symptoms but not necessarily therefore of all subjects who produce dreams). Such a special law might involve the idea that a senseless mental content—for example, a neurotic symptom—is always a compromise formation, alluding at the same time both to mental contents that belong to sequences leading to gratification and to mental contents that belong to sequences leading to avoidance of danger.

This strategy is suggested by the nonstatement view of theory. For relatively accessible explications of the nonstatement view of theory, see Giere (1979b) and Suppes (1967). For more technical explications, see Stegmüller (1976), Suppes (1957), and Van Fraassen (1972). Here, I draw especially on Giere and Stegmüller. As I have tried to make clear in the introduction to this chapter, I, of course, do not mean to claim that the theory of psychoanalysis has reached that stage where it is amenable to the kind of rigorous formalization in terms of set theory described by Stegmüller, Suppes, and Van Fraasen. I do believe that prospects for a more rigorous formulation of psychoanalytic theory might be improved if the strategy I have outlined, which is suggested by the nonstatement view of theory, is followed. Throughout the book, when I suggest ways of defining the theoretical predicate ". . . is a Freudian system," I follow Giere's relatively informal approach (specifying laws that must be true of, if a predicate is to be satisfied by, a domain) rather than Suppes's very formal approach (specifying a set-theoretical structure which a domain must have if a predicate is to be true of it).[2]

## 3. The Nonstatement View of Theory

In the nonstatement view, a theory has the following constituents.

*a*) A *theoretical predicate* (for example, ". . . is a Newtonian particle system"). A theoretical predicate, which is a linguistic entity, is true of a domain if and only if the domain satisfies certain conditions (for example, if and only if a certain set of laws or a certain set of hypotheses are true in that domain). The sets of plants and the sun, and some set of atomic particles in a container of liquid under heat or pressure, are both domains of which the theoretical predicate " . . . is a Newtonian particle system" is true just because Newton's laws are true of each of them.

*b*) An *intended domain* (for example, the planets and sun).[3] The theoretical predicate is formulated with this domain in mind, or the predicate is true of this domain if it is true of any domain. The members of a domain may be idealized abstractions from concrete phenomena; for example, particles (bodies without physical extensions) are members of those domains of which the predicate " . . . is Newtonian particle system" is true.

*c*) A set of *nontheoretic domains*. It is possible that the theoretical predicate may be extended to (may be true of) these domains. The nontheoretic properties of individual members of these domains, or the nontheoretic relations between or among individual members, are designated by pretheoretic or nontheoretic terms. These properties and relations, or the terms designating them, are pretheoretic (commonsensical or intuitive), or are theoretic in some other presupposed theory. (For example, a physical thing has a location—or undergoes a change in location—in space and time.)

That an individual in a nontheoretic possible domain has such a property, or that individuals in the domain exemplify such a relation, are facts to be explained by the theory.

*d*) A set of *theoretic domains* (a subset of the set of nontheoretic domains). The theoretic properties of individual members of these domains, or the theoretic relations between or among individual members, are designated by theoretic terms. These theoretic properties or rela-

2. See technical note 2.

3. A domain is a set of individual entities and the properties such entities may have or relations that may hold between or among them.

tions, or the theoretic terms designating them, distinguish the theory in which they occur from other theories. (Examples are "force" and "mass.")

That an observable or inferred individual in a theoretic domain has such a property, or that individuals exemplify such a relation, has an explanatory function.

*e*) A set of *actual domains* (a subset of the set of theoretic domains). Laws, or hypotheses, stating deterministic or probabilistic relations between or among nontheoretic and theoretic variables, are formulated using the nontheoretic and theoretic terms of the theory. These laws or hypotheses are exemplified by each actual domain. That is, statements of these laws or hypotheses are true in each actual domain. A theoretical predicate is true of a particular domain just in case a set of interrelated but independent laws or hypotheses is exemplified by that domain. (Example: Newton's laws.)

*f*) Sets of *special domains* (subsets of the set of actual domains). Each particular set of special domains exemplifies special laws peculiar to those domains (for example, laws just applicable to elastic bodies or to pendulums).

To explicate a theory, then, is to identify a theoretical predicate, and the domains it is *intended* to be true of, it *may be* true of, and it *is* true of: an intended domain, a set of nontheoretic domains, a set of theoretic domains, a set of actual domains, and sets of special domains.

A theoretical predicate is a conceptual tool. It is used to formulate testable claims about different empirical domains. To use a theoretical predicate is to formulate an empirically testable *theoretical hypothesis*, which claims that a theoretical predicate is true of a particular domain. It is this empirical claim that is tested, and provisionally accepted or rejected as true or false. If such a hypothesis is rejected as false, the theoretical predicate is not therefore necessarily abandoned. It has apparently failed with respect to one application of it. But at least one other application has already been successful (the intended application)—and perhaps other applications also. With each different domain to which the theoretical predicate is shown successfully to apply, the theory establishes its claim to generality.

## 4. The Domains of Psychoanalysis

The predicate " . . . is a Freudian system" is intended to apply to systems of psychological entities, just as the predicate " . . . is a classical Newtonian particle system" is intended to apply to systems of physical entities.

I shall regard the set of psychological entities of a *single subject* as a domain. Any such domain—that is, any subject—is a *possible* domain of psychoanalysis.

The domains of psychoanalysis are often considered to be: the domain of neurotic and psychotic symptoms, the domain of dreams, the domain of parapraxes, the domain of jokes. Following the nonstatement view of theory, we might then have as a theoretical predicate " . . . is a wish-fulfillment structure" and as a theoretical hypothesis "Dreams are wish-fulfillment structures."

However, I shall treat the single subject as an independent domain, and single subjects as the possible domains of psychoanalysis. Of such a domain it is possible to claim "this subject is a Freudian system"— where the statement "A domain is a Freudian system if and only if certain general hypotheses or laws are satisfied by it" is a definition of the theoretical predicate " . . . is a Freudian system." This formulation, as we shall see in the next section, has certain advantages for answering the question "What are the individual entities of a domain of psychoanalysis?" and in conceptualizing single subject research.[4]

## 5. Psychological Entities

At once, we are faced with the difficulty of identifying psychological entities. These are clearly not as easy to identify as physical entities, which have spatiotemporal extension. However, if anything is a psychological entity, then a wish, a belief, a memory, a thought, a perception, or a feeling is a psychological entity. Such terms as "wish," "belief," "memory," "perception," "feeling" are undefined primitives or, more accurately, nontheoretic terms in psychoanalysis, even if they are theoretic terms in some other theory, for example, a theory of psychological capacities.

Are these psychological entities thing-like or event-like? If thing-like they coexist; if event-like they co-occur.[5] Perhaps we should regard them in both ways. A memory of a state of affairs, enduring over time as a more or less permanent registration, is thing-like. That John is aware of a memory of a state of affairs on a particular occasion (John's remembering, John remembers something, he recalls a memory into

4. The choice of single subjects as domains is not indispensible for the position that the nonstatement view of theory is useful in formulating psychoanalytic theory.

5. Reichenbach (1947) distinguishes between domains of things and domains of events. Davidson (1967a, 1967b) describes a way to represent events as individuals which have properties and are related (in particular, causally related) to one another. Vendler (1967) argues, however, that events are caused but that causes are not events.

awareness) is event-like. (That John is aware of a memory may be considered a transient property of the memory.)

If a reader should object to thinking of wishes, perceptions, or thoughts, expressed in noun-form, as entities, because that expression makes these entities sound strangely or unbelievably thing-like, I hope that it is, or that it will become, clear to that reader that I could just as well and essentially equivalently have defined individual entities in a domain of interest to psychoanalysis as the acts of a single subject (such acts as wishing, perceiving, thinking). These entities, then, become event-like rather than thing-like. They may be regarded as events produced by the subject, and as activities of the subject they are, logically speaking, (first-order) attributes of the subject. In turn, these acts have their own attributes. Psychoanalysis, then, would be conceived as investigating (second-order) attributes of these (first-order) attributes of the subject and relations between or among them.

Similarly, one might also, and again I believe essentially equivalently, define individual entities in a domain of interest to psychoanalysis as time-slices of a single subject, and investigate the properties of and relations between and among psychological entities the subject produces on different occasions. Methodologically, one takes a sample of different kinds of acts belonging to one occasion for a cross-sectional study of a single subject, or a sample of different occasions (essentially, then, a sample of acts of the same kind belonging to different occasions) for a longitudinal study of a single subject.

The differences among these formulations are matters of language— merely notational variants—and do not, I believe, have any ontological significance.

*Definitions: Psychological Entities as Representations and Appraisals; Psychological States and Structures*

A psychological entity is a relation between a subject and some state of affairs.

A psychological entity, when it is a perception, an imagining, or a thought, is a subject's representation of a state of affairs, irrespective of its significance for him. For example, he perceives, imagines, or thinks of or about a state of affairs. Such a representation identifies, refers to, designates, names, or describes the constituents of a state of affairs (physical, psychological, social, or cultural entities and properties of or relations between or among such entities).

A psychological entity when it is a belief, a desire or wish, or a feeling, affect, or emotion, is a subject's epistemic, hedonic, or moral appraisal or evaluation of a state of affairs as represented (perceived, imagined, or thought of or about). For example, a subject may believe, on cognitive grounds, or according to cognitive standards or criteria, that a state of affairs obtains or does not obtain in the actual world. He may feel that for him, on hedonic grounds, or according to hedonic standards or criteria, a state of affairs is, was, or would be gratifying (or a means to achieving a gratifying state of affairs), threatening, or thwarting. That is, he wishes-to or wishes-that, he fears-that, or he is angry-that. He may feel that for him, on moral grounds, or according to moral standards or criteria, a state of affairs is obligatory, permissible, or forbidden. This view of affect, feeling, or emotion as an evaluation or appraisal contrasts with Freud's conception of affect as discharge; but it is consistent with Freud's conception of the signal functions of such emotions as anxiety and guilt.[6]

A *psychological state* of a single subject is defined (identified, individuated) by the superset of the subject's coexisting or concurrent sets of attitudes (such as wishes, beliefs, memories).[7]

A *psychological structure* is a set or sequence of different kinds of psychological entities, which are interrelated. A neurotic symptom, a dream, a parapraxis: each—whatever differences there may be between them—is a set of interrelated psychological entities, and therefore a psychological structure.

## Qualitative and Quantitative Measurements of the Properties of Psychological Entities

Scientists want to investigate what relations exist between the properties of individual entities in a domain. So, in a domain of psychological entities, a scientist investigates what relations exist between properties of psychological entities. Therefore, a scientist must be able to describe a psychological entity qualitatively or quantitatively.

Both representations and appraisals can be described quantitatively (on an "ordinal scale" at least) as well as qualitatively, although Freud tended to consider representations as having primarily qualitative dimensions and appraisals as having primarily quantitative dimensions.

6. Compare with Rapaport (1953). See, also, for some interesting ways of thinking about affect, feeling, or emotion: Arnold (1970), Davitz (1970), Leeper (1970), Miller et al. (1960), Peters (1970), and Pribram (1970, 1971).

7. Federn (1952, especially pp. 210–226) seems to have had some such idea as this when he referred to ego states and the repression of such states.

Perceptions, fantasies, or thoughts, for example, may be more or less vivid (more or less detailed); or more or less definite (more or less vague) with respect to the degree to which constituents of states of affairs which are mentioned are unequivocally identified or have clear referents. Affects, feelings, or emotions may involve more or less physiological arousal, or a greater or lesser degree of mobilization of physiologically grounded resources. They may be more or less intense or peremptory, may involve more or less of a tendency, inclination, or impulse to act to bring about, to remove, to avoid, or to prevent a state of affairs. A subject may be more or less confident of his competence or ability to bring about, to remove, to avoid, or to prevent a state of affairs according to his evaluation of it.

In every case, a belief, emotion, or moral evaluation is always an appraisal of the degree of significance a state of affairs has for the subject: how confident he is in his belief that a state of affairs does or does not obtain in the actual world; how satisfying, threatening, or thwarting for him he assesses a state of affairs to be; how strongly he is committed to realizing a moral imperative to bring about or avoid a state of affairs.

## *How Are Psychological Entities Individuated?* [8]

How can a scientist, seeking to discover what relations exist between psychological entities or their properties, tell one psychological entity from another? How can he tell when two apparently different pyschological entities are the same?

A psychological entity is a subject's relation to or attitude toward a state of affairs. First, it is individuated by specifying which *subject* is in that relation to—or has that attitude toward—a state of affairs. Second, it is individuated by specifying what kind of relation to—or *attitude* toward—a state of affairs it is. Third, it is individuated by specifying the *state of affairs* to which a subject has a particular kind of relation or toward which he has a particular kind of attitude. A sentence that for the believing, wishing, perceiving subject designates or describes a state of

---

8. The rest of section 5 is devoted to a consideration of some of the consequences, the felicities and infelicities, of choosing psychological entities as the "individuals" in the domains of interest to psychoanalysis. It is addressed to the reader who is especially interested in general in conceptual analysis, and in particular in such problems as the individuation of entities in a domain—that is, how do we identify one psychological entity in such a way as to distinguish it from another? A reader may proceed to section 6 of this chapter (pp. 93–96) without loss of continuity.

affairs he believes, wishes, or perceives, can be used, therefore, to individuate a psychological entity.[9]

States of affairs may or may not obtain in the actual world.[10] They are described by such phrases as "the killing of Jim by Joe" (this state of affairs is the sequence "Kills, Joe, Jim"); "the seduction of Jane by Jeremy" (this state of affairs is the sequence "Seduces, Jeremy, Jane"). Clearly, the order of the entities exemplifying the relation makes a difference: "Jim kills Joe" designates a different state of affairs than "Joe kills Jim."[11]

Constituents of states of affairs are, in the context of the theoretical interests of psychoanalysis, to be taken as they are designated, named, or described by a subject. In other words, these constituents are to be identified or individuated by the predicates (designating properties and relations), and by the names and descriptions (designating entities exemplifying such properties and relations), that for a subject represent the constituents.

## Psychological Entities as Signs

A psychological entity can be regarded as a sign of a state of affairs. A psychological entity may be an *indexical sign*. A perception is an indexical sign of a state of affairs. A psychological entity may be an *iconic sign*. A pictorial image, an imagining, or a fantasy is an iconic sign of a state of affairs. A psychological entity may be a *symbolic sign*. A thought is a symbolic sign of a state of affairs.[12]

An index functions as a sign by pointing to an existent state of affairs; it points to the state of affairs because it is existentially or actually connected to it. Index and state of affairs are spatiotemporally contiguous,

9. For discussions of ways to identify or individuate the objects of so-called propositional attitudes such as wishes and believes, see Davidson (1968–1969), Kaplan (1968), Quine (1953, 1955, and 1979), and Scheffler (1963, especially pp. 88–110). Also, see technical note 3.

10. See technical note 4.

11. For discussions of states of affairs as the designata of sentences and as the objects of propositional attitudes such as wishes and believes, see Barwise and Perry (1981), Marcus (1981), and Taylor (1976).

12. For Peirce's theory of signs, see Buchler (1940), Feibleman (1946), and Wiener (1958). See, also, the discussion of symbolic function in Edelson (1971), terminology in semiology and a theory of signs in Edelson (1972), and the differences between presentations and representations in Edelson (1975).

are related as cause and effect (are members of the same causal chain), or are related as part and whole of an existent object or event.

An icon functions as a sign by evoking for a subject a state of affairs, which may or may not obtain in the actual world; it evokes the state of affairs because the subject perceives or comprehends that one resembles the other. Icon and state of affairs share one or more properties, or have the same structure or form. That is, icon and state of affairs belong to at least one class in common, or corresponding elements in each have the same kind of relation to each other.

A symbol functions as a sign by designating a state of affairs, which may or may not obtain in the actual world; it designates a state of affairs because it describes it or refers to it by a convention, or by using the syntactic, semantic, and phonetic rules of a language known to the subject. There need be no resemblance between symbol and state of affairs; in this sense, the relation between them is arbitrary.[13]

## *Bringing in the "Real World"*

What about the "real world"? Does this conceptual strategy, as described so far, deprive the psychoanalyst of a language in which he can explain the properties of and relations between and among psychological entities by referring to properties of and relations between or among actual states of affairs in the world? Does it result in total concentration on psychic reality? How, then, does one make use of concepts like "secondary process" and, more important, such notions as that a psychological entity does not make sense, that a feeling is inappropriate, that a perception is hallucinatory? All of these seem to rely on a matter-of-fact reference to things as they are.

I shall introduce the actual world by remembering Freud's early discussion (1900, pp. 565–566) of a wish as having the aim of producing a "perceptual identity" ("a repetition of the perception which was linked with the satisfaction of the need"). Thus, instead of saying that a subject wishes to do such-and-such, we could say that a subject wishes that a particular state of affairs (in which he does such-and-such) obtains in

---

13. Similarly, one state of affairs may be an indexical, iconic, or symbolic sign of another state of affairs. If an index, both states of affairs are existent and connected irrespective of any mediation by a knowing subject. A state of affairs functions as an icon of another state of affairs only if, for some knowing subject, the states of affairs resemble each other or have the same structure or form. A state of affairs functions as a symbol of another state of affairs only if, for some subject, the constituents of the state of affairs are elements of a language whose rules the subject knows.

the actual world, and we could say that this wish is gratified when he perceives this state of affairs (perceives himself doing such-and-such). Since a perception is an index of an existent state of affairs, that a wish is gratified implies that a wished-for state of affairs obtains in the actual world.

I shall regard a "hallucinatory perception" as an *imagining* (Wollheim, 1979), not a perception, which under certain circumstances the subject may believe to be a perception and which under these circumstances may serve at least temporarily as a surrogate or substitute for a perception.

In addition, we could describe an action as involving a relation between a subject and a state of affairs—the subject "originates" a state of affairs. One might say about a subject "he does it"—where "it" refers to the state of affairs which includes his action as a constituent. Such an assertion (that he does it) would also, of course, then imply that the state of affairs including his action obtains in the actual world.

### Some Additional Problems

Additional questions might be raised concerning this way of dealing with the definition of the entities which belong to domains of interest to psychoanalysis. How does one perspicuously speak or write of complex states of affairs (for example, states of affairs involving logical connectives or relations between states of affairs)? Consider, for example, the psychological entity suggested by such a sentence as "Jack believes (that Jane hates her father *but* loves Jack)." How does one perspicuously speak or write of states of affairs which are themselves psychological entities? "Jack believes (that he *wishes* to kill Jim because Jim wishes to kill him)." What if a constituent of a state of affairs is an element which a subject cannot name or describe? "John wishes (that there were *someone* who loved him)."

### 6. The Pretheoretic or Nontheoretic Concepts of Psychoanalysis

What are the nontheoretic properties of and relations between or among psychological entities? What terms do we use that, even if they are theoretic terms in some other theory, are pretheoretic or nontheoretic in psychoanalytic theory?

First of all, a psychological entity or a psychological structure (a set of interrelated psychological entities) does or does not make sense, or makes more or less sense than another psychological entity or psychological structure. Perceptions, memories, wishes, beliefs, feelings, and thoughts do or do not make sense; or one perception, memory, . . . or thought may make more or less sense than, respectively, another perception, memory, . . . or thought. Neurotic symptoms, dreams, and parapraxes, in general, do not make sense; or one neurotic symptom, dream, or parapraxis may make more or less sense than another. It is no accident that Freud's title to Lecture XVII of the *Introductory Lectures on Psycho-Analysis* is "The Sense of Symptoms."

Whether a psychological entity or structure does or does not make sense, or that one psychological entity or structure makes more or less sense than another, can be determined independently of any knowledge of psychoanalytic theory. That a psychological object or structure does or does not make sense, or that one psychological entity or structure makes more or less sense than another, is a fact to be explained by psychoanalysis.

In a classical Newtonian particle system, a physical object remains in a state of constant motion unless a force intervenes to change its motion. It is change in its motion that requires explanation. Analogously, psychological entities or the psychological structures formed of them make sense unless some "force" (a causally efficacious factor) interferes. It is that (or the extent to which) a psychological entity does not make sense that requires psychoanalytic explanation.

The analogy here to a physical system does not imply a physicalist or reductionist view of psychological phenomena, or a concern to make psychology a natural science. The entities in the two domains differ (physical entities vs. psychological entities). The properties and relations of entities in the two domains differ (for example, changes in an an entity's motion in one vs. whether or not an entity makes sense in the other). However, the scientific enterprise is the same in both cases: formulating hypotheses about a domain and using probative evidence to choose between such a hypothesis and rival or alternative hypotheses.

"Making sense," of course, is a pretheoretic or nontheoretic term. (No knowledge of psychoanalytic theory is required to apply it.)

A psychological entity or structure makes sense when it is apparent that it is *purposive*. It is governed by, or oriented to, a purpose. It is a step on the way to an end or goal. It belongs to a sequence of psychological entities or structures that starts with a wish to bring about a desired state of affairs and terminates with a perception of that state of affairs.

A psychological entity makes sense when it is *intentional*. A subject identifies himself as the agent who has an attitude toward a state of affairs. He does not disown an attitude toward a state of affairs that at the same time he manifests or implies he has.

A psychological entity or structure makes sense when it is apparent that it is *rational*. It is rational if a subject has adequate grounds for his belief that it is necessary in order to produce, or increases the probability of producing, a desired state of affairs.

A psychological entity makes sense when it is apparent that it is *appropriate*. It is appropriate if it is a member of a psychological state; it is an appraisal of a state of affairs; other psychological objects which are also members of that psychological state provide grounds, reasons, justification, or explanation for the saliency, persistence or recurrence, or intensity of this appraisal; and it is compatible with other appraisals. "Saliency," "persistence," and "intensity" have to do with the degree of success a psychological entity has in competing with other psychological entities for access to such resources as consciousness, attention, and the motor apparatus; or with the strength, resistance to change, or causal impact of a psychological entity.

A psychological entity makes sense when it is apparent that it is *logical*. It is logical if it is a member of a psychological state, and what it implies about some state of affairs (for example, that the state of affairs obtains in the actual world) is compatible with what other psychological entities that are members of that psychological state imply.

A psychological entity makes sense when it is apparent that it is *reality-adapted*. That it is reality-adapted comes into question if it is an improbably fixed or stereotyped representation or appraisal of ambiguous states of affairs (even though these permit different representations or appraisals), which recurs despite dysfunctional consequences with respect to the avowed goals, purposes, aims, or desires of a subject.

For example, a psychological entity does not make sense if it has no apparent relevance with respect to achieving any wished-for state of affairs, and no apparent relation to other psychological entities, and a subject cannot prevent himself from producing it. A psychological entity, originating an action, does not make sense if a subject believes that the action is a means to achieving a wished-for state of affairs but has no grounds or has inadequate grounds for this belief, or in fact has grounds for believing the action is inimical to achieving that wished-for state of affairs, and he cannot prevent himself from carrying it out. A psychological entity, a feeling, does not make sense if a subject longs for a state of affairs which he has no grounds for feeling will be pleasurable or which he in fact has grounds for feeling will disgust him, if he is frightened by or angry about a state of affairs when he can detect no threat or thwart in it, or if the intensity of his fear or anger is clearly disproportionate to whatever degree of actual threat or thwart he believes to be present. A psychological state does not make sense if one psychological entity implies that a state of affairs obtains in the actual world, and another psychological entity implies it does not or cannot obtain in the actual world, or that some other state of affairs, logically incompatible with the first, coexists with it in the actual world.

Psychoanalytic theory is distinctively concerned with explaining or accounting for the fact that a psychological entity (or structure, or state) does not make sense (that is, is nonpurposive, unintentional, irrational, inappropriate, illogical, or reality-maladapted) when:

*a*) some state of a unique physical system, and some state of a unique biological system, and some degree of psychological capacity are necessary conditions for the realization or production of that entity (structure, state);

*b*) but no specific defect in or traumatic disruption of that physical system, and no specific fault in the design or organization of that biological system, and no permanent innate deficiency of that psychological capacity, and no specific feature of some external environment or specific information or lack of information in that environment is either a necessary or sufficient condition for, or cause of, the fact that the psychological object or structure does not make sense.

Such terms as "purposive," "intentional," "rational," "appropriate," "logical," and "reality-adapted" are pretheoretic or nontheoretic terms in psychoanalysis. To make a judgment that on the face of it a psychological entity is purposive (or nonpurposive), intentional (or unintentional), or rational (or irrational) does not require a knowledge of psychoanalytic theory, although it may require a knowledge of other theories.

"Conflict" is also a pretheoretic or nontheoretic term in psychoanalysis; it does not take knowledge of psychoanalytic theory to recognize a conflict. A psychological structure is a conflict if and only if it includes the following interrelated constituents:

*a*) a wish;

*b*) a fear;

*c*) a belief that the achievement of a wished-for state of affairs—or of another state of affairs necessary for the achievement of the wished-for state of affairs—is sufficient to produce, or has a strong propensity to result in, a perception of a feared state of affairs; and

*d*) a counterwish to prevent the wished-for state of affairs (more precisely, a counterwish to bring about some state of affairs which is believed to be necessary or sufficient to avoid, or has a strong propensity not to be followed by, the wished-for state of affairs).

## 7. The Theoretic Concepts of Psychoanalysis

That a psychological entity or psychological structure lacks to one degree or another access to consciousness is a theoretic characterization of such an entity or structure. A nontheoretic domain of psychological entities is also a theoretic domain of psychoanalysis, if its members can be characterized in terms of the degree to which they are permitted to achieve access to consciousness or the extent to which they are prevented by obstacles from achieving access to consciousness.

Other theoretic terms, applicable to, or true or false of, psychological entities or structures in theoretic domains of psychoanalysis include: "instinctual," "gratified," "fulfilled," "derivative."

In 1915, Freud explicated what he meant by *instinct*. "If now we apply ourselves to considering mental life from a *biological* point of view, an 'instinct' appears to us as a concept on the frontier between the mental and the somatic, as the psychical representative of the stimuli originating from within the organism and reaching the mind, as a measure of the demand made upon the mind for work in consequence of its connection with the body" (pp. 121–122).

That subjects perceive bodily states and that such perceptions have causal efficacy constitute the minimum content of the so-called biological or instinct-theoretical aspect of psychoanalysis. I assume that those who are uncomfortable about what they consider the excessive biological cast of Freud's thought are not inclined to abandon either element of this minimum content.

On the other hand, it is also important to note that it is the "psychical representative" of the state of the body and not the state of the body itself that has causal efficacy. We are not here directly studying a physiological system or an organism as a physical body, and there is an important difference between the state of that system or body and the perception the subject has of its state. Even though the two are causally connected, they are not identical.

An instinctual wish or impulse is the sign of a hypothetical central state or process in a biological system. This central state or process is cyclical in intensity, and variations in its intensity may occur independently of, but may also be in response to, changes in a subject's external environment. An instinctual wish is *peremptory* (it preempts resources such as attention); it *persists* until the subject acts successfully to create the state of affairs which gratifies it; it *recurs* irrespective of vicissitudes of the relation between the subject and his external environment.

If a subject wishes to perform an action, and does perform the action, the wish is said to be *gratified*. If a subject wishes to perform, and does not perform, but instead imagines performing, an action, and if his imagining this performance satisfies certain conditions and especially if it is accompanied by the belief that he is perceiving rather than imagining, then the imagining of the performance serves temporarily as a surrogate or substitute for the perception of it and the wish is said to be *fulfilled*.

A *derivative* of an unconscious instinctual wish is the result of a more or less distorting transformation of the unconscious instinctual wish. The kind of change effected by a transformation of an unconscious instinctual wish as well as the number of transformations of it determine how distorted a derivative is, and therefore how little sense it makes. In generating a derivative, any transformation may be used repeatedly.

No matter what kind of psychological entity a derivative of an instinctual wish is, and no matter how distorted it is, it will retain to some degree some of the same properties, and enter into some of the same kind of relations, as the instinctual wish—recurring periodically and frequently, claiming attention, and (if the derivative itself is some kind of, but not necessarily an instinctual, wish) attracting capacities, time, and effort to its realization, which might otherwise have been committed to gratifying the instinctual wish.

Examples of transformations and derivatives in a specified domain (the set of psychological entities produced by John) are: [14]

*a*) John's wish becomes John's belief.

*b*) John's wish becomes John's fear.

*c*) An "I love him" kind of psychological entity becomes an "I hate him" kind of psychological entity.

*d*) An "I hate him" kind of psychological entity becomes a "he hates me" kind of psychological entity.

*e*) An "I love him" kind of psychological entity becomes an "I love her" kind of psychological entity.

*f*) John's wish, a "she loves me" kind of psychological entity, becomes John's belief "that I love her is her wish."

*g*) Regressive objects (persons, parts of persons, or things required for the gratification of instinctual wishes in an earlier developmental epoch), or persons or things which allude to, represent, or are identified with such regressive objects, are substituted for nonregressive objects.

*h*) An instinctual wish, which is regressive (had primacy in an earlier

14. For some examples of Freud's, see Freud (1911, especially pp. 62–65).

developmental epoch) and to which the subject has a fixation, is substituted for a frustrated instinctual wish (having primacy in a later developmental epoch).

A subject has a *fixation* to some particular regressive instinctual wish if and only if either a perception of an obstacle to the gratification of some other wish, or competition of different wishes for resources, has a strong propensity to result in the subject turning to, or (when he allocates resources) giving priority to, that particular regressive instinctual wish.

A fixation results from an interaction between unfavorable childhood experiences and inborn characteristics of a subject's biological system. That is, the strength of a fixation is a function of the product of the degree to which childhood experiences are unfavorable and the degree to which an inborn property of a subject's biological system is present. The degree to which it is present may be indicated by the strength of a subject's propensity to achieve a certain kind of pleasurable body state more easily than another, or to feel a certain kind of body state as more pleasurable than another.

## 8. The Intended Domain of Psychoanalysis

Freud's hypothetical baby can be regarded as the beginning of the development and explication of a theoretical predicate and the choice of an intended domain.[15]

A hungry baby screams or kicks helplessly. But the situation remains unaltered, for the excitation arising from an internal need is not due to a force producing a *momentary* impact but to one which is in continuous operation. A change can only come about if in some way or other (in the case of the baby, through outside help) an 'experience of satisfaction' can be achieved which puts an end to the internal stimulus. An essential component of this experience of satisfaction is a particular perception (that of nourishment, in our example) the mnemic image of which remains associated thenceforward with the memory trace of the excitation produced by the need. As a result of the link that has thus been established, next time this need arises a psychical impulse will at once emerge which will seek to recathect the mnemic image of the perception and to re-evoke the perception itself, that is to say, to re-establish the situation of the

15. The way in which a metaphor or "model" like this one is used in the development of a scientific theory, with Freud's use of metaphor as the exemplar, has been explicated by J. Edelson (1983).

original satisfaction. An impulse of this kind is what we call a wish; the reappearance of the perception is the fulfillment of the wish; and the shortest path to the fulfillment of the wish is a path leading direct from the excitation produced by the need to a complete cathexis of the perception. Nothing prevents us from assuming that there was a primitive state of the psychical apparatus in which this path was actually traversed, that is, in which wishing ended in hallucinating. Thus the aim of this first psychical activity was to produce a 'perceptual identity'—a repetition of the perception which was linked with the satisfaction of the need. [Freud, 1900, pp. 565–566]

Any set of psychological entities produced by a single subject, some of which may not make sense (or which form psychological structures that may not make sense), is an intended domain of the theoretical predicate " . . . is a Freudian system." This predicate, if it is true of any domain, is true of such domains when the psychological entities or structures that do not make sense are neurotic symptoms. Neurotic symptoms are always peremptory and irrational, and do not belong to any conscious purposive sequence.

Freud argued in effect that the predicate " . . . is a Freudian system" should also be extended to such domains when the psychological entities or structures that do not make sense are dreams. Dreams are often illogical and incomprehensible, and do not belong to any conscious purposive sequence.

Freud also argued in effect that this same predicate should be extended as well to such domains when what does not make sense is a parapraxis, such as a slip of the tongue or pen, or a forgetting. A parapraxis is a miscarriage or failure of mental functioning. That is, it is an apparently inexplicable production of, or inability to produce, a psychological entity or structure, when that production or failure of production interrupts, aborts, or constitutes an obstacle to, the execution of a conscious purposive sequence or the achievement of a consciously desired goal.

Interestingly enough, such apparently inexplicable interruptions of, or obstacles to, achievement of the consciously desired goal of communicating whatever comes to mind to the psychoanalyst, unhampered by conscious decisions to select certain contents over others or to pass some contents and censor others, must be counted as—although they are not usually called—parapraxes. It is this sort of parapraxis, along with the analysand's explicable conscious reluctance to communicate certain contents, which have become the primary focus of attention and investigation in the psychoanalytic treatment process.

The analysand's reluctance, of course, is not strictly speaking a parapraxis until such time he perceives it as inexplicable. He may find, for example, he can no longer account to his own satisfaction for his reluctance solely by referring to its membership in conscious purposive sequences, or he may find that, even if he understands the reasons for his reluctance and regards these reasons as unimportant compared to his reasons for overriding it, he is still unable to override it.

## 9. Sketch for a Definition of the Theoretical Predicate " . . . Is a Freudian System"

A formulation of the theoretical predicate " . . . is a classical Newtonian particle system," where location in space and time, velocity, and acceleration are nontheoretic concepts, and mass and force are theoretic concepts, might look something like the following (Giere, 1979b).

A domain is a classical Newtonian particle system if and only if it satisfies the following laws (that is, if and only if these laws are true in the domain):

 *a*) Newton's first law (constant motion),

 *b*) Newton's second law (force acting on a body),

 *c*) Newton's third law (equal and opposite action and reaction).

A domain of psychological entities produced by a single subject is a Freudian system if and only if it satisfies the following "laws" or hypotheses (that is, if and only if these "laws" or hypotheses are true in the domain):[16]

 *a*) Any psychological entity produced by the subject is purposive (that is, belongs to at least one goal-oriented sequence of psychological entities).

Anything that weakens commitment to, or that diminishes access to

---

16. Again, I emphasize that here I follow Giere's relatively informal strategy for defining a theoretical predicate in terms of the laws which must be true of a domain satisfying the predicate, rather than the strategy of Suppes, for example, who would specify in set-theoretical terms what kind of structure of sets, relations, and functions a domain must be if a predicate is to be true of it.

The term "laws" is to be taken very loosely in this discussion of psychoanalytic theory, as mainly a marker for laws which eventually will have to be rigorously formulated, and which so formulated will be recognized as conforming to the criteria statements must satisfy to be considered scientific laws. What these criteria are is a matter I shall not go into here.

resources for, the execution of conscious purposive sequences results in an increasing dominance in mental life of psychological entities belonging to unconscious purposive sequences.

A psychological entity is produced only if some instinctual wish or impulse is above threshold intensity. If an instinctual wish or impulse reaches threshold intensity, and no obstacle interferes with its gratification, then this wish or impulse results without delay in a perception of the state of affairs which, according to memory, previously gratified it. The perception of this state of affairs in turn reduces the intensity of the instinctual wish or impulse below threshold intensity.

A hypothetical condition in which no instinctual wish or impulse is above threshold intensity, or no obstacle delays gratification, involves a scientific idealization. That is to say that achieving such a condition can occur only in a domain of psychological entities that has no members. In other words, it cannot occur in any domain of interest to us. We do not expect to encounter such a condition, although we may approximate or extrapolate it by reducing the magnitude of obstacles to gratification, or by observing states in which instinctual wishes or impulses are relatively quiescent. Similarly, the conception of a hypothetical condition in which no force acts upon a body, so the body continues in a state of constant motion, is an idealization. We do not expect to encounter this condition either, though we may approximate or extrapolate it by reducing the magnitude of acting forces.

*b*) IF (1) the subject is executing or traversing a goal-oriented sequence, *and* (2) the termination of the sequence is the gratification of a wish or impulse, *and* (3) an obstacle prevents the subject from reaching the termination of the sequence,

THEN the subject's propensity to imagine the gratification of the wish or impulse and, by imagining the gratification of the wish or impulse, to fulfill it, increases. Fulfillment of the wish or impulse in imagination decreases, at least transiently, the subject's propensity to attempt to execute or traverse the sequence terminating in gratification, or to some relatively slight extent his propensity to commit resources to such attempts. Since the wish or impulse, although fulfilled in imagination, remains ungratified, so long as the obstacle to gratification persists, attempts at wish-fulfillment will recur.

If an instinctual wish or impulse reaches threshold intensity, and there is delay (more or less extended) before any perception of the gratifying state of affairs occurs (if it does occur at all), then during this delay the following psychological entities are produced: an appraisal of the non-gratifying state of affairs (affect), and an imagination of the gratifying state of affairs. Imagining the gratifying state of affairs (for example, a fantasy, dream) substitutes, or acts as surrogate, for a perception of the gratifying state of affairs. Imagining, like perceiving, a gratifying state of affairs is capable of reducing the intensity of the instinctual wish or impulse, although in most cases to a lesser extent and even then only briefly.

Since the subject has finite resources (attention, time, effort) to commit to producing these three kinds of psychological entities (fantasies, affects, perceptions), if more resources are committed to achieving one of them, fewer resources are available for achieving others. The sum of propensities attached to these possible outcomes of an instinctual wish, therefore, tends to be constant. If the propensity to produce one outcome increases, the propensity to produce other outcomes decreases, accounting in part at least for the impression psychoanalysts have that some quantity is constant or conserved. (This may be in part why psychoanalysts find it necessary to speak or write of psychic energy, a constant amount of libido, or conservation of energy in the distribution of ego-libido and object-libido—that is, in addition to their attempt to do justice to the quantitative aspects of psychological entities.)

The extent of the different contributions of primary and secondary processes to imagining a state of affairs depends in part on the relative priority given, at different periods of development and in different ego-states, on the one hand, to merely imagining a gratifying state of affairs and, on the other hand, to imagining a state of affairs that is believed to be a means to reaching a gratifying state of affairs, when such imagining is a preparatory or anticipatory step in an attempt to achieve ultimately a perception of that means state of affairs.

*c*) IF (1) the subject's body, in relevant respects, is physically intact and functioning without impairment, *and* (2) the subject's environment cannot be held to account for any incapacities in psychological functioning in question, *and* (3) the subject produces a psychological entity or structure that does not make sense (for example, he does not recognize it as belonging to any goal-oriented sequence of psychological entities accessible to consciousness), *or* (4) the subject's production of, or inability to produce, a psychological entity or structure interrupts, aborts, or constitutes an obstacle to the execution of a conscious purposive sequence or the achievement of a consciously desired goal, but does not itself make sense (for example, his production of, or inability to produce, such an entity or structure does not itself serve any conscious purpose),

THEN (1) what does not make sense is related directly to (belongs to), or is related by primary process indirectly to, at least one goal-oriented sequence of psychological entities which the subject is executing or traversing, *and* (2) this direct or indirect relation, or that the subject is executing or traversing this sequence, or some or all of the sequence itself, is inaccessible to consciousness, *and* (3) at least one such sequence has as its termination the gratification of a sexual or hostile impulse or wish, whose origin is in infantile life, when it was indicated by and found fulfillment in one or more fantasies now inaccessible to consciousness, *and* (4) that sexual or hostile impulse or wish is a constituent in an intrapsychic conflict, some or all of which is inaccessible to consciousness.

Anything that weakens commitment to, or that diminishes access to resources for, the execution of a sequence terminating in the avoidance of danger, when that sequence is a constituent of an unconscious intrapsychic conflict, results in strengthening commitment to, or mobilization of resources for, the execution of a sequence terminating in the gratification or fulfillment of a sexual or hostile wish or impulse, when that sequence also is a constituent of the unconscious intrapsychic conflict.

The effective strength of an instinctual wish or impulse is a function of: (1) (cyclic?) changes in the subject's propensity to execute the sequence terminating in the gratification or fulfillment of the wish or impulse, changes which occur essentially independently of the subject's environment, but which are enhanced or mitigated by changes in the subject's environment (the presence or absence of external excitations, inducements, temptations, opportunities); and (2) the strength of counterwishes (noninstinctual wishes to prevent by one means or another the gratification of the instinctual wish or impulse), which are instigated by affects signaling that danger is attendant upon such gratification or fulfillment.

Every increase in the strength of an instinctual wish that is a constituent of an unconscious conflict, relative to the strength of a counterwish, decreases the degree of distortion of derivatives of the instinctual wish, and increases the saliency, persistence, or intensity of such derivatives.

Every decrease in the degree of distortion of these derivatives, and every increase in their saliency, persistence, or intensity, increases the intensity of such affects as anxiety or guilt.

Every increase in the intensity of such affects as anxiety or guilt increases the strength of the counterwish.

Every increase in the strength of the counterwish increases the degree of distortion of derivatives of the instinctual wish, or the extent to which these derivatives are denied access to consciousness, or decreases the saliency, persistence, or intensity of such derivatives.

Every increase in the degree of distortion of derivatives of the instinctual wish, or the extent to which these derivatives are denied access to consciousness, or decrease in the saliency, persistence, or intensity of such derivatives, decreases the intensity of such affects as anxiety or guilt.

Any unconscious conflict is, therefore, activated by an increase from any cause in the strength of an instinctual wish that is a constituent of that conflict, relative to the strength of a counterwish that is a constituent of the same conflict. Such activation produces changes in the occurrence, frequency, or intensity of neurotic symptoms or parapraxes, which result from the various tendencies or processes mentioned and which (therefore) do not (to some extent) make sense.

In Chapter 11 of this book, I shall discuss how Luborsky in effect— although he does not discuss what he is doing in this way—tests a theoretical hypothesis claiming his single subject is a domain that is a Freudian system (as I have just defined the theoretical predicate " . . . is a Freudian system").

## 10. The Science of Imagination

The "laws" I have stated in this tentative version of a definition of the theoretical predicate " . . . is a Freudian system" are rough indicators of, or placeholders for, what such laws might eventually look like.[17] Obviously, I am not here claiming that development of these three kinds of laws in particular, or their use in a definition of a theoretical predicate such as " . . . is a Freudian system," would constitute an adequate formalization of psychoanalytic theory. I merely suggest the form that a

17. Formulations by Rapaport (previously cited) and by Freud (most centrally, *The Interpretation of Dreams*, and then *Introductory Lectures on Psychoanalysis*, 1916–1917, and here most especially the masterly Lecture XXIII "The Paths to the Formation of Symptoms") have clearly influenced my version of a possible definition of the theoretical predicate " . . . is a Freudian system."

formalization of psychoanalytic theory might take in the framework of a nonstatement view of theory.

My list of "laws" or hypotheses is of course far from exhaustive and does not include many important ideas that could rather easily be culled from the existing corpus devoted to psychoanalytic theory. However, I find it hard to believe that ultimately among such laws there will not be laws that:

*a*) define a condition (purposiveness? making sense?) such that any apparent or actual departure or deviation from it calls for explanation;

*b*) distinguish between conscious and unconscious purposes;

*c*) show how conscious mental contents are related to, or are derivatives of, unconscious mental contents;

*d*) define an attempt to gratify a wish or impulse as an attempt to reinstate as a perception what is merely a memory of a past perception of gratification;

*e*) explicate under what conditions—for example, the frustration of attempts at gratification—an attempt to achieve a perception of past gratification is expressed in acts of imagination or wish-fulfillment;

*f*) attribute, in any effort to explain what does not make sense, explanatory, determinative, or causal status to (1) unconscious sexual and hostile wishes or impulses (whose origin is, in the form of fantasy, in infantile mental life); and (2) unconscious intrapsychic conflicts, whose constituents include such wishes or impulses, as well as fears of harm believed to be attendant upon, in actuality or fantasy, the gratification or fulfillment of such wishes or impulses, and attempts to prevent, deprive access to consciousness to, or transform and distort, even the imagined fulfillment of such wishes or impulses.

My adumbration of a definition of the theoretical predicate ". . . is a Freudian system" suggests a view of psychoanalysis as a science of the imagination.[18] In this view, psychoanalysis is not primarily a general psychology, encompassing all human capacities or "behavior" (Edelson, 1977). Psychoanalysis studies action insofar as action flows from, or is determined by, imagination. Its primary interest is not in accounting for rational action, but in accounting for psychological entities or structures that do not make sense, by tracing the vicissitudes of instinctual wishes in successful, unsuccessful, interrupted, aborted, or distorted wish-fulfillments.

18. See Edelson (1978) for an apposite discussion of Lionel Trilling's "psychoanalysis is a science of tropes" and Wallace Stevens's "psychoanalysis is a science of illusions."

Questions by philosophers of science about psychoanalysis are not necessarily informed by this view of psychoanalysis as the science of the imagination. Furthermore, such questions are often couched in a way suggesting that very far from the philosopher's mind indeed is the recognition that:

*a*) sexual fantasies (and fantasies about the body, its parts and functioning) occupy a large realm in mental life;

*b*) conscious as well as unconscious struggles over masturbation and especially over the fantasies associated with masturbation are ubiquitous in mental life;

*c*) relationships with siblings as well as parents appear and reappear in manifold guises in conscious and unconscious imaginings;

*d*) struggling against homosexual and sadistic wishes or impulses (especially), whenever these wishes or impulses are stirred up, is determined and persistent in imagination as well as action;

*e*) ambivalence about doing or being done to, making it happen or letting it happen, taking it in or spitting/pushing it out, acting independently of or turning to/leaning on another, thrusting in or opening up, provide recurrent themes for and the tropes of our discourse with ourselves and others; and

*f*) all of these are expressed in psychoanalytic treatment in an efflorescence of ideas, feelings, and fantasies about the psychoanalyst.

One forgets that what an analysand is ultimately willing to express and reveal in the psychoanalytic situation is not, at least in the form in which it appears there, otherwise accessible. It is not public shared knowledge of what goes on all the time in a person's head. It is not commonsense, nonliterary, nondistanced knowledge of everyday life. But it can be conscious. Fantasies in which anything goes, disguised to some extent (but not always very much) under the pressure of scruples or realistic considerations, are the most personal secrets (kept even, to some extent, from oneself). Nevertheless, no matter how much one looks away or attempts to ignore or isolate these fantasies, they along with similar unconscious contents determine in unknown ways and to a varying extent one's relations with the actual world. It is the ubiquity and the power of the fantastical which frequently eludes philosophical discussants of psychoanalysis.

It is surely more important for the psychoanalytic investigator to document the mundane details of such phenomena convincingly, in an organized way, forcefully, vividly, and explicitly, distinguishing phenomena sharply and clearly from theoretical formulations about them, than to preoccupy himself with pilpul. However, these are phenomena the psychoanalyst takes for granted, and his hypotheses about them appear to him to be self-evident. He often does not seem to take seriously that what to him and to his colleagues is self-evident, if it is to be scientifically credible as well, requires a cogent argument, according to the canons of scientific reasoning, about the relation between his hypothesis and his evidence.

# 7 An Examination of the Supposition That Testing Psychoanalytic Hypotheses Is Ultimately Dependent Upon Developments in Neural Science

Those who follow Grünbaum in seeing no possibility of testing psychoanalytic hypotheses in the psychoanalytic situation might be tempted to propose some sort of relation between psychoanalytic theory and theories about the brain or physiological organism, such that psychoanalytic theoretic hypotheses could be indirectly tested by testing experimentally theoretic hypotheses about the brain or physiological organism. One might suppose, for example, that these two theories were parallel or isomorphic. One might also, alternatively, think that psychoanalytic theory (for example, in its definition of the predicate " . . . is a Freudian system") should include hypotheses about relations between nontheoretic physiological and psychological variables. Envisaging such possibilities as these, there are those who believe that psychoanalytic theory must include at least references to hypothetical states of the brain and to neurophysiological processes, or that psychoanalytic theory must at least be formulated so that work in the neural sciences is capable of falsifying it, casting doubt upon it, or forcing revision of it.

That psychoanalysis must respond to new findings in neural science (and to theoretical formulations about these findings) by revising Freud's theory of dreams is the burden of two much-debated recent papers (McCarley and Hobson, 1977; Hobson and McCarley, 1977). I shall note here, somewhat digressively, that despite the appearance of these papers in a well-refereed, well-edited journal, the account given in them of Freud's theory of dreams is mistaken in a number of ways. The authors misattribute to Freud such ideas as that memories cause dreams and that day residues or endogenous visceral stimuli produce dreams. In their preoccupation with explaining *dreaming*, they overlook entirely Freud's avowal that he is primarily interested in interpreting the form and content of *dreams* as "psychical structures," which have a "meaning and which can be inserted at an assignable point in the mental activities of waking life" (Freud, 1900, p. 1), and that he is not interested in explaining dreaming regarded as a neurophysiological state or event. Indeed, he disavows any intent to deal with physiological problems, in-

cluding the problem of sleep, "even though one of the characteristics of
the state of sleep must be that it brings about modifications in the conditions of functioning of the mental apparatus" (p. 6). (See, also, in this
connection, Edelson, 1972.)

Rubinstein (1976) proposes solving the problem of selecting among
competing general clinical hypotheses, each one of which in conjunction with the analysand's reports accounts for some clinical observations, by allowing the fit or lack of fit between general clinical hypotheses and scientifically credible neurophysiological hypotheses to make
the selection. He argues (1967, pp. 65–66) that "one function of the
metapsychological hypotheses [of psychoanalysis] is to justify the presupposition of central states and processes on which the explanatory
power of . . . higher-level clinical hypotheses rests." (Higher-level
clinical hypotheses are here assumed to refer to actual entities and their
relations.) "Now, to justify these presuppositions the metapsychological
hypotheses must be confirmed *independently* of their clinical confirmation." Rubinstein concludes that this can occur only if the metapsychological hypotheses are confirmed neurophysiologically, which requires
that a neurophysiological interpretation be given to theoretical terms in
psychoanalysis. These "terms must be so defined that they may *conceivably* have neurophysiological referents."

It will be clear from what follows in this chapter that I do not agree
with the positions taken by either Hobson and McCarley or Rubinstein.
I hold rather that psychoanalysis should be prepared to argue that the
development of theories of mind and brain has not advanced anywhere
near the point where one could reasonably claim it is even possible for a
proposition about the mind and a proposition about the brain to contra-
dict each other. The nonstatement view of theory suggests, at least to
me, that development of a theoretical predicate about mind and a theoretical predicate about brain, each with intended applications in its
own quite different set of possible and actual domains, can and should
be carried on independently, at least at this point in history. Neither is
likely for a long time, if ever, to be a source of logical challenge to the
other. Attempts to make it appear otherwise should be viewed with sus-
picion as hegemonic. Efforts to tie psychoanalytic theory to a neurobiological foundation, or to mix hypotheses about mind and hypotheses
about brain in one theory, should be resisted as expressions of logical
confusion.

I see no reason to abandon the position Reiser (1975) takes despite his avowed belief in the "functional unity" of mind and body, when he considers the mind-body relation:[1]

> The science of the mind and the science of the body utilize different languages, different concepts (with differing levels of abstraction and complexity), and different sets of tools and techniques. Simultaneous and parallel psychological and physiological study of a patient in an intense anxiety state produces of necessity two separate and distinct sets of descriptive data, measurements, and formulations. There is no way to unify the two by translation into a common language, or by reference to a shared conceptual framework, nor are there as yet bridging concepts that could serve . . . as intermediate templates, isomorphic with both realms. For all practical purposes, then, we deal with mind and body as separate realms; virtually, all of our psychophysiological and psychosomatic data consist in essence of covariance data, demonstrating coincidence of events occurring in the two realms within specified time intervals at a frequency beyond chance. [P. 479]

I think it is at least possible that scientists may eventually conclude that what Reiser describes does not simply reflect the current state of the art, methodologically, or the inadequacy of our thought, but represents rather something that is logically or conceptually necessary, something which no practical or conceptual developments will ever be able to mitigate.

## 1. Theoretical Predicates and Isomorphism

The idea of a theoretical predicate can be used to characterize a relation between domains as isomorphic (Suppes, 1957, pp. 254, 260–271). If a theoretical predicate designates an abstract structure of sets and relations or functions of a certain kind, without regard to how these are interpreted by different domains, then two very different domains (their members are very different kinds of individuals) may have the same structure. That is, they are isomorphic. For example, a domain of numbers and arithmetical operations performed upon numbers, on the one hand, and a domain of physical objects and actions upon or procedures involving these objects, on the other, may be said to be isomorphic. That such domains are isomorphic justifies applying numbers

---

1. Although recently he seems to be moving away from this position (personal communication).

to things. "What we can do is show that the structure of a set of phenomena under certain empirical operations and relations is the *same as* the structure of some set of numbers under certain arithmetical operations and relations" (Suppes, 1957, p. 266).

It does not matter what particular sets and relations constitute each different domain. So long as each set and each relation in one domain corresponds to or matches a set or relation of the same general kind in the other domain, the same theoretical predicate is true of each domain. The two domains are isomorphic or have the same structure. For example, if each pair of individuals in one domain is related (for example) by a binary symmetric relation, and for each pair of individuals in one domain there is a corresponding pair of individuals in another domain, and each corresponding pair of individuals in the other domain is also related by a binary symmetric relation, then the two domains are isomorphic—although the entities in one domain are very different in kind from the entities in the other domain, and the relations are different (though they are of the same general kind, that is, binary and symmetric). Similarly, if each pair of individuals, one from one set and the other from a second set in a domain, are related by a one-to-one function, and, for each such pair, a corresponding pair of individuals (though of a very different kind), one from one set and the other from a second set in another domain, are also related by a one-to-one function, then the two domains are isomorphic.

## 2. Are the Domains Mind and Brain Isomorphic?

One approach to a "solution" of the so-called mind-brain problem starts with the claim that a theory of mind can be reduced to a theory of brain because psychological and physical-biological domains are isomorphic. This is a claim that at the least for every pair of individual entities in a psychological domain (whatever these entities may be), which are in some relation to each other (whatever the relation is), there is a corresponding pair of individual entities in a physical-biological domain (whatever these very different entities may be), which are in some relation to each other (whatever that very different relation is), and that the relation in one domain is the same kind of relation (for example, binary and symmetric) as the relation in the other domain. If a theoretical predicate designates the structure of a domain, then in this case it might be successfully applied to both these isomorphic domains.

I have previously noted that McCarley and Hobson (1977) and Hobson and McCarley (1977) claim that a revision of Freud's theory of dreams is required by new findings (and speculations about these) in the neural sciences. They justify this claim by assuming that mind and brain are isomorphic domains.

In order to reject this claim, at least insofar as it is justified in this way, I shall define two theoretical predicates (" . . . Generates a Dream" and " . . . Generates a $D$-Sleep State"), which might conceivably be regarded as competing with one another, or instead as interchangeable or logically equivalent to each other. The first predicate is intended to apply to a mind as a domain; the second is intended to apply to a brain as a domain. The definitions of these predicates are:

  *a*) $X$ Generates a Dream if and only if $S$.

  *b*) $Y$ Generates a $D$-Sleep State if and only if $T$.

In place of $X$: some set of specified organized or related constituents, constituting a structure called a mind. A dream is an object a mind generates on some occasion.

In place of $Y$: some set of specified organized or related constituents, constituting a structure called a brain. $D$-sleep is a state of a brain on some occasion.

In place of $S$, a characterization of a dream as having a set of nontheoretic features; and an explanation of each feature in terms of nontheoretic and theoretic properties of or relations between or among the constituents of a mind.

In place of $T$, a characterization of a $D$-sleep state as having a set of nontheoretic features; and an explanation of each feature in terms of nontheoretic and theoretic properties of or relations between or among the constituents of a brain.

What is the relation between these two theoretical predicates? Suppose that $A$ and $B$ are, respectively, the mind of a specified subject regarded as a psychological entity and the brain of that same subject regarded as a physical organism, and that $P$ and $Q$ are, respectively, the theoretical predicates " . . . Generates a Dream" and " . . . Generates a $D$-Sleep State."

  *a*) It may be that $P$ is true of $A$ if and only if $Q$ is true of $B$. This formulation is consistent with the belief that *mental predicates are reducible to physical predicates*. (Since "if and only if" is symmetrical, this formulation is also consistent with the belief that physical predicates are reducible to mental predicates.) Such a belief does not require that $A$ and $B$ be isomorphic domains.

  *b*) *It may be true that A and B are isomorphic domains*. $A$ and $B$ are isomorphic domains if and only if:

(1) for every constituent of $A$, there is a corresponding constituent of $B$;

(2) a constituent of $A$ has a certain property if and only if the corresponding constituent of $B$ has a certain property (the property of the constituent of $A$ is not necessarily the same property as the property of the constituent of $B$);

(3) a pair of constituents of $A$ are in a certain relation if and only if the corresponding pair of constituents of $B$ are in a certain relation (the same kind of relation, but not necessarily the same relation); and

(4) for every nontheoretic feature of a dream explained in terms of properties of and relations between or among constituents of $A$, there is a corresponding nontheoretic feature of a $D$-sleep state (not necessarily the same feature) explained in terms of properties of and relations between or among corresponding constituents of $B$.[2]

Of course, if these domains are isomorphic and if an explanation of a feature of a $D$-sleep state is falsified and needs to be revised, then the explanation of the corresponding feature of a dream may need to be revised. However, if these two domains are not isomorphic, a revision of neural science theory will not necessarily require a revision of psychoanalysis.

If *the domains A and B are isomorphic*, then *the theoretical predicate P is reducible to the theoretical predicate Q*. Both these claims are strong.[3] Neither is made by Freud (despite Hobson's and McCarley's assertions to the contrary). At the most, Freud asserts or implies that $Q$'s being true of $B$ is a necessary condition for $P$'s being true of $A$. He did find it heuristic to consider a conception of the nervous system as a model in developing his conception of the mental apparatus, but he nowhere asserts or implies that the two are isomorphic in the systematic sense just described.[4]

Indeed, the assumption of an isomorphism of this sort appears to be

2. Hobson and McCarley give the impression they think that, if two domains are isomorphic, properties, relations, or features in one domain are the same (rather than different but the same general kind) as corresponding properties, relations, or features in the other domain.

3. Both the claim made by the italicized antecedent, and the claim made by the italicized consequent, of the preceding conditional.

4. The notion that the content of psychoanalytic theory logically depends in some way on, and is logically equivalent to, Freud's quasi-neurophysiological "Project," which after fruitful conceptual play he discarded, has been frequently questioned by M. Reiser (in personal communications). He is correct. One does not use the origin of a hypothesis (context of discovery) as grounds for accepting or rejecting it (context of justification).

as implausible as the assumption that there must be some statement in the language of physics that will account for the fact that a sundial, a clock, and an hourglass all "tell time" (Dennett, 1978). That there are different physical realizations which have the same use, function, or consequence suggests that emergent concepts, not required for physics, are required to explain machines or biological systems (whose parts are arranged to achieve certain tasks, ends, or outputs, each of which contributes to a final task, end, or output), and by extension that more than one physical realization is consistent with a particular state of, or event in, a psychological system.

The theories of neural science and psychoanalysis have different domains and different nontheoretic concepts. Both neural scientist and psychoanalyst take the body in its aspect as a physical system which obeys the laws of physics for granted. Neither is concerned with testing these laws. The theoretic terms of physics are nontheoretic terms in biological theory. The theoretic terms of biology are nontheoretic terms in a theory of psychological capacities presupposed by psychoanalytic theory. The facts neural science and psychoanalysis intend to explain are radically different and the problems they want to solve are on quite different levels.

Even if the assumption of isomorphism were true, that assumption is no guide to what revisions must be made in one theory as a consequence of revisions in the other. What entities in one domain do correspond to what probably very different kinds of entities in the other domain? There should be at least one relation in each domain such that one of the relations holds between a pair of entities in one domain if and only if the other relation holds between a corresponding pair of entities in the other domain. How are the two relations, which are probably very different even if of the same general kind, to be identified? One can be sure that superficial analogies will not help here.

Certainly, there is no possibility of demonstrating that mind and brain are isomorphic, unless each kind of theory achieves a much more mature, rigorous, precise formulation than is now in sight.

*c) Weaker, more plausible, and easier-to-demonstrate claims about the relation between mind and brain* are that:

(1) $P$ is true of $A$ on an occasion only if $Q$ is true of $B$ on that occasions; or

(2) $P$ is true of $A$ on an occasion only if $Q$ is true of $B$, or $M$ is true of $B$, or $N$ is true of $B$, on that occasion; or

(3) $P$'s being true of $A$ on an occasion increases the likelihood of $Q$'s

being true of $B$ on that occasion. This claim is equivalent to the claim that the successful application of a particular mental predicate and the successful application of a corresponding physical predicate to different aspects of the same organism on the same occasion are statistically associated or correlated.

Theoretical predicates can be considered to compete if and only if they can be applied to the same set of nontheoretic possible domains (both theories make use of the same set of nontheoretic terms), and there is a subset of actual domains of which both are true. One of these predicates will then be accepted instead of the other if it has greater generality—if there are some actual domains of which it is true and the other is not true. Clearly, mental and physical theoretical predicates such as $P$ and $Q$ do not satisfy the required conditions, and therefore cannot be considered to compete with one another.

## 3. Psychoanalysis and the Mind-Brain Problem

The psychoanalyst takes it for granted that there is a biological mechanism which works, which is capable of producing the phenomena in which he is interested. The neural scientist wants to investigate and explain this capacity. The distinction between a physical system, a biological capacity, and a psychological performance, and what it takes to explain each, is fundamental (Chomsky, 1972; Dennett, 1978).

In the instance of a dream, for example, it is possible to take the biological mechanism (the arrangement of parts, the sequence of subsystems with interdependent inputs and outputs), which has dreaming as an ultimate output, for granted. The fact that the mechanism is working is taken for granted. It is also possible to take for granted that some physical state or body, a physical system obeying laws of physics, is intact. A particular state of the physical system is perhaps one, but not the only possible, physical realization for the mechanism which is designed to produce dreaming as an output to have. (Remember the sundial, hourglass, clock.)

Assuming only an intact physical system, the neural scientist is interested in the biological mechanism for dreaming, in the nature of the design which is realized in the physical system. What makes dreaming possible? How does dreaming work? How is dreaming done? How can this capacity be explained?

Assuming an adequately designed mechanism (it works, it does or produces what it is designed to do or produce), which is realized in some way in an intact physical system, the psychoanalyst is interested then in what particular wishes or beliefs are manifested by a dream. What wishes and beliefs must be attributed to the dreamer to account not for dreaming but for the content and form of a particular dream? Taking the capacity to dream for granted, the psychoanalyst inquires how a purposive performance on a particular occasion, which calls upon and manifests the capacity, is to be explained.

The two problems are very different. If psychoanalysis concerns itself at all with the problem of the biological system or working mechanism, which I very much doubt, it might be in its so-called metapsychology. Metapsychology from this point of view could then be considered a statement in a psychological language of a blueprint, or a set of specifications, of the kinds of functions or tasks that must be carried out or achieved by the organism's parts, arranged in a particular way, if dreaming is to take place. The neural scientist ought to find the predicted parts and arrangements. Metapsychology, if this were true of it, would be a ticket which would be cashed in by the neural scientist, not the psychoanalyst. (I believe this account to be true, if at all, of only a small part of metapsychology.)[5]

Accepting the formulation that theoretical predicates are true of domains or systems, then, in an explication of the "mind-brain relation" I shall say that the predicate " . . . is a biological system" presupposes the theory of physical systems, which is unproblematic for it. This predicate takes concepts from physical theory (for it, nontheoretic concepts) and uses such nontheoretic concepts in describing the entities of a domain of interest to it or stating the facts to be explained by it.

The predicate " . . . is a sign-receiving, sign-generating, and sign-interpreting system" presupposes biological theory, which is unproblematic for it. This predicate takes concepts from biological theory (for it, nontheoretic concepts) and uses such nontheoretic concepts in describing the entities of a domain of interest to it or stating the facts to be explained by it.

The predicate " . . . is a rational (psychological) system" presupposes a theory of sign systems, which is unproblematic for it. This predicate takes concepts from such a theory (for it, nontheoretic concepts) and uses such nontheoretic concepts in describing the entities of a domain of interest to it or stating the facts to be explained by it.

The "mind-brain" problem arises because of the different stages of development of these theories, and lack of clarity about the relations

---

5. This seems to be Rubinstein's position, which is stated earlier in this chapter.

between them. It is usually not apparent how a change in one theory will affect another theory, which depends upon the first for its non-theoretic concepts, and therefore for its statement of the facts it will attempt to explain. It is even less apparent how modifications in one theory will affect any one of a number of other theories, each one of which depends upon another for its nontheoretic concepts and, therefore, for its statement of the facts to be explained by it. In this view, such theories as these are related hierarchically (in a nested arrangement), rather than isomorphically.

From this point of view, a person as a concrete object may be considered analytically in one aspect a physical system, in another aspect a biological system, in another aspect a psychological system, and in still another a member of a social system. That is, such a concrete object may be conceived as the organizer or integrative focus of different domains.[6] Each domain has as members a certain kind of entity (particles, molecules, needs, roles)—which are described by a different set of nontheoretic and theoretic terms—and each domain exemplifies a different set of fundamental laws.

It is possible that each of these domains, regarded as a functional system, is analyzable into simpler subsystems, of the same kind as itself, which interact to make a more complex system. Each of these subsystems are analyzable in turn into simpler sub . . . subsystems. The process ends at the level of analysis where the sub . . subsystem of a particular kind of system can equally well be described as another kind of system. For example, a biological system may be analyzable into simpler sub . . . subsystems, each one of which has the characteristics of a biological system, until at some level the sub . . . subsystem can equally well be described as a physical system or a domain of physical particles (Dennett, 1978).

Since physical, biological, psychological, and social theories refer to different kinds of entities, use different nontheoretic and theoretic terms to explain different kinds of facts, and make different empirical claims in applying different theoretical predicates, each such kind of theory can only be considered a rival of another theory of the same kind of system (physical, biological, psychological, or social, respectively). The request for a biological explanation of psychological facts is incoherent, unless what is meant is such a fine analysis "from the top

6. This is the position taken by T. Parsons in developing his theory of action (Edelson, 1976).

down" that what results are sub . . . subsystems of psychological systems, which at this level of analysis have lost the characteristics of psychological systems and can be equally well or better regarded as biological systems. At the next level "up" these biological sub . . . subsystems interact in such a way that they constitute a system which is describable as a psychological system. We are a long way from such an analysis, either from the "top down" or from the "bottom up."

An argument that a theory of neural science is to be preferred over a psychological theory is not an empirical claim about the actual world that is true or false; evidence has no relevance here. The argument expresses competing values—for example, a preference for studying one kind of domain rather than another, or a guess about the relative payoffs from each kind of study at a particular point in time (with the "state of the art," available methodology, and opportunities for success and advancement in mind).

An argument that a theory of neural science better explains "the facts" than a psychological theory only appears to be but is not an argument about which theory should be accepted provisionally rather than the other as true on evidential grounds. What set of "facts" could both theories appropriately offer to explain? An argument actually claiming that if a theoretical predicate of neural science is true of a domain, then a "psychological" theoretical predicate cannot or is not likely to be true of that domain must involve some confusion about what domain it is that is being studied. What kind of domain is it to which both predicates might appropriately be applied?

Even a debate about decisions to use one set of nontheoretic or theoretic terms rather than another in describing or explaining facts in a particular kind of domain is not a debate about an empirical question. So, also, the definition of one theoretical predicate cannot be argued as more likely to be true or false than another such definition. Definitions are not statements about the world, which are true or false, but conceptual inventions.

When Freud states, "It is *self-evident* that dreams must be wish-fulfillments, since *nothing but a wish can set our mental apparatus at work*" (1900, p. 567, italics mine), or "No influence that we can bring to bear upon our mental process can ever enable us to think without purposive ideas" (1900, p. 528), he has made a conceptual decision to study domains to the elements of which the terms "wish" and "purposive" can be applied. (These are nontheoretic or pretheoretic terms in psychoanalytic theory.) He has not made in the assertions beginning "nothing but a wish" and "no influence" any empirical claim—he has made no statement that is true or false—about such domains. (Whether he is correct in assuming that, given these decisions, it *logically* follows that dreams are wish-fulfillments is another matter.)

Similarly, many of the neo-Freudian revisions of psychoanalytic theory cannot be empirically refuted. They appear, rather than empirical claims, to be proposals—for example, to restrict the set of domains chosen or intended to satisfy a theoretical predicate which is psychoanalytic. For example, the so-called social or interpersonal schools propose—certainly H. S. Sullivan did propose—to limit this set of domains to those constituted by persons and interactions between persons.

In discussing the mind-brain problem, it is important to distinguish between *external questions*, concerning, for example, the choice of a frame of reference, and *internal questions*, concerning, for example, the choice of one rival empirical claim over another when both claims are made within the same frame of reference. In his 1950 paper "Empiricism, Semantics, and Ontology," Carnap (1956, pp. 205–221) makes a similar distinction. Writing about the acceptance of a kind of entity or linguistic expression, he emphasizes the difference between external questions "concerning the existence or reality of the total system of the new entities" (p. 214) and internal questions about the truth or falsity of statements made in an accepted language or "way of speaking."

In testing theoretical hypotheses, we try to answer internal questions about a domain. The invention of a theoretical predicate, the choice of a domain that is the intended application of a theoretical predicate, or the decision to study one kind of domain rather than another, raises external questions.

Questions about the choice of a kind of domain for study or the choice of a way to characterize entities in a domain are not questions that can be decided by collecting evidence. However, a question about whether a theoretical predicate is or is not true of a domain is a question about the actual world and can in principle be empirically decided.

PART **3**

# The Response

I shall now respond directly to Grünbaum's formidable argument. Although Grünbaum claims to confine himself in his critique to Freud's writings, I shall in my response certainly refer to developments in psychoanalysis that are not present or focal in, but which follow upon, Freud's work. Grünbaum does not hesitate to quote other psychoanalysts to buttress his arguments. If he does in fact confine his critique to the way in which Freud only among psychoanalysts carried out and reported his work, he limits that critique more than I think he intends to do.

Here, I do not take issue with Grünbaum's basic assumptions about the scientific enterprise, his adherence to the correspondence theory of truth, for example. I address rather in particular his assertion that it is *in principle* impossible to test hypotheses in the psychoanalytic situation. I take him to assert, in other words, that it is *impossible* to obtain evidence in that situation, according to the canons of eliminative inductivism, warranting provisional acceptance of a hypothesis over some rival hypothesis. I assume the phrase "testing hypotheses in the psychoanalytic situation," implies the use of data obtained in the psychoanalytic situation, whether that involves, for example, the scoring by judges of the content of transcripts of psychoanalytic sessions (for example, Luborsky, 1967, 1973), or the kind of reasoning a psychoanalyst might use in the psychoanalytic session, exemplified, for example, in Glymour's (1974, 1980) explication of the Rat Man case.

I do not intend, by casting doubt on Grünbaum's assertion, to imply that psychoanalytic investigators actually obtain such truly probative evidence very time they claim to confirm empirically psychoanalytic hypotheses in the psychoanalytic situation. Nor do I expect, even if psychoanalytic investigators should be persuaded it is possible to obtain such evidence, that they will find it easy—or will necessarily be inclined to make the effort—to do so. I also do not intend, by maintaining it is in principle possible to test psychoanalytic hypotheses in the psychoanalytic situation, to imply that extraclinical or experimental testing of psychoanalytic hypotheses is therefore dispensable. Nor do I now, in accepting the usefulness of extraclinical or experimental tests, intend to imply that clinical or nonexperimental testing of psychoanalytic hypotheses is therefore unnecessary.

In brief, I shall question Grünbaum's interpretation of the canons of eliminative inductivism; he seems to consider these canons to be identical with what is actually only one method for satisfying them—*experimental* research, in which a comparison between or among *groups of subjects* is made, in such a way that *all* known relevant variables are controlled.[1] I shall question as well his belief that the data obtained in the psychoanalytic situation are irretrievably contaminated by suggestion, the selection bias of the psychoanalyst, the analysand's preconceptions, and the fallibility of the analysand's memory. I shall argue that it is possible to explicate more precisely than has been done the objectives of psychoanalytic treatment, and, although this will not be any easier for psychoanalytic therapy than for any other psychotherapy, possible also to assess whether in a particular case such objectives have been achieved. Finally, in what I consider to be a decisive refutation of Grünbaum's assertion, I shall show that psychoanalytic hypotheses not only can be but in fact have been tested in the psychoanalytic situation.

---

1. Grünbaum also apparently accepts epidemiologic research, even though it is non-experimental, as potentially capable of testing psychoanalytic hypotheses according to the canons of eliminative inductivism. However, here too, even when there is no experimental manipulation of causal variables by the investigator, the desiderata he implies are that the study should be prospective, not retrospective, and should involve group comparisons and control of extraneous variables. His acceptance of nonexperimental epidemiologic research makes no difference to my response, to the extent this response is directed to Grünbaum's apparent belief that adequate tests of psychoanalytic hypotheses not only involve, when possible, experimental manipulation of causal variables, but always involve in any case group-comparison and control of relevant variables.

# 8    Does Adherence to Scientific Canons Necessarily Require an Experimental Methodology?

Grünbaum is unreasonably stringent in suggesting that the canons of eliminative inductivism can be met only through *experimental* research, that such experimental research in turn must involve a comparison between or among *groups of subjects*, and that in every study *all* known relevant variables must be controlled.

## 1. Must Studies Be Experimental in Order to Obtain Evidential Support for a Hypothesis?

First, although I agree with Grünbaum about the importance of causal hypotheses, it is also true that other kinds of hypotheses may be of importance to a scientist and, therefore, to a psychoanalytic investigator (Bunge, 1979, pp. 255–262). Such hypotheses might make statements about: a structure's properties, a stochastic system's intrinsic propensities to manifest states or events (an example is the postulated cyclicity of instinctual drives), taxonomic associations (that is, relations between or among properties), relations between dependent variables (for example, between two different responses, performances, or productions of the same subject, such as a self-representation and an ideal-representation), or trends (for example, changes in propensities to manifest states or events over time, changes in capacities over time, or developmental trends in general).

Second, *nonexperimental* research and nonexperimental or experimental *single subject* research can be used to test causal hypotheses. Grünbaum argues as if manipulation of an independent variable is essential to obtain data that have relevance to causal hypotheses; and, by manipulation, he means especially the use of different treatment groups, or treatment and control groups, to which subjects have been assigned (ideally, randomly), so that each group can be exposed by the investigator to a different treatment or condition, or to different levels of a treatment.[1]

1. "Treatment" does not necessarily refer to therapeutic intervention but may be any explanatory factor, influence, intervention, property, or condition under study.

*a*) However, typically, data obtained in the psychoanalytic situation are nonexperimental. Causality can be argued, according to the canons of eliminative inductivism, from nonexperimental data by using, for example, causal modeling and statistical controls (Asher, 1976; Blalock, 1961, 1969; Cook and Campbell, 1979; Watson and McGaw, 1980).

*b*) Causality can be argued, according to the canons of eliminative inductivism, from single subject data, if, for example, multiple measurements under baseline (no-treatment) and treatment conditions, or multiple measurements under different treatments or conditions, are obtained for comparison (Hersen and Barlow, 1976).

Grünbaum, when he refers to single subject research, argues as if the only possibility is an "on-off" intervention-baseline–intervention-baseline kind of design. He then supposes that this design is irrelevant to evaluating the efficacy of psychoanalysis because the long duration of the intervention makes it very difficult to eliminate alternative explanatory candidates that might be supposed to account for any effect observed. Other designs are available, however, including the time-series design with a single intervention, which may have a lasting effect, and the equivalent materials design (designs 7 and 9 described by Campbell and Stanley, 1963); as well as the multiple baseline design (which Grünbaum clearly sees is the prototype for cases like Anna O., where it implicitly serves as the basis for the argument that one is justified in eliminating a general placebo effect as an alternative explanation of the effects of the "talking cure" on different symptoms, because these symptoms are affected separately or independently).

That a multiple baseline design is not in principle inapposite to hypothesis testing in the psychoanalytic situation, despite changes in the theory since the case of Anna O. was written, is suggested by the following characteristics of psychoanalytic treatment, among others. For long periods anyway, a particular focal conflict may be the focus of analytic work (Luborsky and Mintz, 1974). "Working through" (roughly, interpreting the manifestations of the same conflict in one context after another) is an important aspect of psychoanalytic treatment.

There is every reason to believe that such designs as these can be used in single subject research to test psychoanalytic hypotheses in the psychoanalytic situation, although not necessarily those hypotheses focused on etiology or therapeutic efficacy with which Grünbaum appears to be especially concerned. Even with respect to these hypotheses, it is possible that etiologic hypotheses can be tested indirectly, by testing hypotheses deduced from them. If, for example, variations in the intensity of an unconscious conflict result in variations in severity or frequency of a symptom, that could be argued to be indirect though incomplete evidence for the role of unconscious conflicts in the *genesis* of neurotic symptoms. The work of Luborsky (1967, 1973) and Luborsky and Mintz (1974) is especially important with respect to this point, and I shall discuss it in greater detail in Chapter 11.

## 2. Must *All* Known Relevant Variables Be Controlled in Every Study?

It is not necessary for psychoanalysis to submit to what seems to be a counsel of perfection. Does Grünbaum imply that all known plausible alternative explanations of an outcome must be eliminated or controlled in every research? I cannot think so. Better for the psychoanalyst to adopt the strategy of seeking in every research to eliminate at least one plausible alternative explanation, the one he sees as a truly plausible alternative, whose challenge most concerns him, and which in a particular study he is able to eliminate. Works on quasi-experimental design are apposite here (Campbell and Stanley, 1963; Cook and Campbell, 1976, 1979), and so is the Group for the Advancement of Psychiatry (GAP) report on controls (1959). Campbell and Stanley argue that if a number of independent and different kinds of studies are tests of a particular hypothesis, and each study eliminates different alternative explanations of the credibilifying outcome, then it is more parsimonious to assume that the truth of the hypothesis accounts for this outcome in each study than to assume instead that in each study a different alternative explanatory candidate accounts for it (pp. 36–37).

Of course, the converging studies must be independent and different in some way (different investigators, methods, settings, subjects). If one adopts this strategy, one accepts that a psychoanalytic hypothesis cannot be tested in the psychoanalytic situation alone, and so one employs various kinds of studies, of children as well as adults, experimental as well as nonexperimental. In referring to the necessity of using a variety of approaches, it is well to call attention to Platt's injunction, given in his presentation of the strategy of strong inference (1964), not to depend upon or become overattached to a particular method of investigation.

Turning to other kinds of studies does not imply that studies in the psychoanalytic situation are dispensable, however. Making inferences from direct observation of children's behavior to psychological processes, for example, contrary to the impression sometimes given, is subject to many of the same kinds of problems that making inferences about the mind of the analysand from his reports is. Experimental studies, just because of the control exerted to exclude extraneous influences, are often problematic with respect to generalization of findings. Furthermore, intervening in an experimental situation, for example, to exacerbate symptomatology in order to test a critical hypothesis, poses immense and perhaps unsolvable practical and ethical problems.

## 3. Alternative Hypotheses Are Not Necessarily Plausible

Not all alternative hypotheses suggesting explanations for an observed outcome other than the one offered by an investigator are necessarily plausible. A psychoanalytic investigator should not be deterred from arguing in a study that a particular alternative hypothesis is not plausible, or from attempting to rule out in "nondesign" ways alternative interpretations of data, when these alternatives are threats to validity—that is, threats to acceptance of the conclusion that the investigator's hypothesis accounts for the outcome he has obtained.

It should not be forgotton that experimental design is only one way to rule out alternative interpretations [of data] and that sometimes threats [to validity] can be ruled out in nondesign ways. This is especially the case when particular threats seem implausible in light of accepted theory or common sense or when the threats are validly measured and it is show in the statistical analysis that they are not operating. [Cook and Campbell, 1979, p. 96]

According to Cook and Campbell (p. 96), three factors in case studies in the social and clinical sciences often serve the same role (eliminating alternative explanations of an outcome) that pretest measures and control groups serve in formal experimental designs:

*a*) Often, many different variables are measured after a subject has been exposed nonexperimentally to a treatment or condition in order to assess the effect of that treatment or condition.[2]

*b*) "Contextual knowledge is already rich, even if impressionistic."

*c*) "Intelligent presumptions can be made" about what the subject would have been like without exposure to the treatment or condition.[3]

---

2. "It may even be that in hypothesis-testing case studies, the multiple implications of the thesis for the multiple observations available generate 'degrees of freedom' analogous to those coming from numbers of persons and replications in an experiment" (p. 96).

3. For Cook and Campbell, a single group, exposed to a treatment and measured on outcome variables posttreatment, is the subject here.

However, one would often recommend with the case study that scholarly effort should be redistributed so as to provide explicit evidence about conditions prior to the presumed cause and about contemporary conditions in social settings without the treatment that are similar to the setting in which the case study is taking place. All inference is comparative, and it is usually optimal to have comparable sorts of evidence, comparable degrees of detail and precision, about conditions prior to the implementation of a treatment and about factors that occur simultaneously with the treatment.
[Pp. 96–97]

Support for causal inference in a case study may be provided by either of the following circumstances (pp. 97–98):

*a*) A hypothesis entails that different outcome variables will have different levels, and they do.

*b*) An effect is observed, which is rare (information is available about the probability of its occurrence), and for which there are few if any known causes other than the presumed cause (well-established causal hypotheses exist to justify this conclusion); and spatiotemporal contiguity links the subject to that cause.

## 4. Two Goals: Obtaining Support for Hypotheses Versus Falsifying Hypotheses

Even if one were to accept the canons of eliminative inductivism as providing the best basis for arguing the relation between hypothesis and evidence, one might adopt a weaker goal than achieving support for, or what Grünbaum calls "scientific credibilification" of, a hypothesis.

A psychoanalyst, for example, might seek, rather than to obtain confirmations of or support for the hypotheses he believes to be true, at least to get rid of false hypotheses. Then he will proceed by deducing a consequence of a hypothesis to be tested. This consequence is likely on background knowledge or another plausible hypothesis (which also may be and in most cases will be a psychoanalytic hypothesis) to be false. If this expected consequence does in fact fail to be the case, he can confidently regard the tested hypothesis as false and congratulate himself on having rid the world of still another false idea. (He still faces in some cases at least the problem of obtaining his data in such a way that he can argue that the consequence failed to be the case because the tested hypothesis is false, and not because the operation of other factors brought about this outcome, though the tested hypothesis is true.)

Such an investigator carries out the task of weeding so that plants in a garden can grow. A small set of hypotheses will survive this process of weeding out the unfit; these hypotheses remain possibly true. Without satisfying the canons of eliminative inductivism, the investigator is not warranted in going so far as to claim that they are scientifically credible. Nevertheless, his achievement, though minimal with respect to obtaining evidential support for any hypothesis, is not minor.

Wisdom (1967) argues in this connection that two facts tend to give weight to suggestion as a plausible alternative explanation of the effects of therapeutic intervention in psychoanalysis. One fact is that different conclusions are reached by different "schools of therapy." A second fact is that each school gets associations that confirm its theories. Both these phenomena, he points out, result from following procedures that aim at obtaining or enumerating mere confirming instances (on the mistaken notion that these give evidential support) rather than seeking refutations or falsifications.

Is there any reason to believe that the strategy of obtaining falsifications is in principle impossible in the psychoanalytic situation? It would appear not. No one can doubt that a marked increase in the number of single subject researches carried out by psychoanalytic investigators that decisively refute empirical claims following from at least some psychoanalytic hypotheses would greatly enhance the scientific status of psychoanalysis.

# 9    Are the Data Obtained in the Psychoanalytic Situation Really Irretrievably Corrupt?

I question Grünbaum's claim that there is no way of separating contaminated from uncontaminated data in the psychoanalytic situation.

## 1. Data Are Necessarily Theory-Laden

In any research one must provisionally accept some data statements as true in order to test any hypotheses at all (Glymour, 1980; Popper, 1959a). What the analysand infers as a cause does not have to be included among such data, nor even what he purports to remember—but certainly, unless there is some evidence the analysand intends consciously to deceive, his conscious feelings, thoughts, beliefs, and perceptions can be included among such data.

Of course, these data are theory-laden, but the theory with which they are laden is not psychoanalytic theory, and with respect to psychoanalytic theory such data are nontheoretical facts. As in any science, one can for reason ultimately question the truth of the data statement itself, but that does not mean there are no data statements that can be accepted at all. As Glymour points out, if one wishes to be especially cautious here, one can use as relatively indisputable nontheoretical data, not what the analysand refers to in his statements, but that the analysand reports what he reports.

## 2. Suggestion

There can be no question of minimizing or dismissing the problem of suggestion in the psychoanalytic situation. Freud himself took the problem of suggestion very seriously, as Grünbaum (1980, pp. 320–321; 1982b) points out. It might be possible, however, to reduce the adulteration of data by suggestion in the psychoanalytic situation—perhaps to a vanishingly small degree, or at least to a degree it ceases to be a *plausible* alternative explanatory candidate. Many features of the psychoanalytic situation, in contrast to those of other psychotherapies, are in fact designed to control extraneous external influences on the analysand's productions. The disciplined use of psychoanalytic technique which focuses on interpreting defense, rather than providing the analysand with suggestions about what he is defending against, also might cast doubt on a claim that suggestion is a plausible alternative explanation for an outcome observed in a particular single subject research.[1]

In general, while an analysand may achieve insight into the nature of an unconscious conflict and its effects, interventions by the psychoanalyst which enable the analysand to achieve such insight do not necessarily do so by stating for him what the unconscious conflict or its constituents are. Many "interpretations" merely infer the analysand is having difficulties saying what is on his mind, point to the contexts in which he has such difficulties, or call attention to what is to be explained—for example, stereotypy in the images the analysand conveys from session to session, or in the way he resolves ambiguities in the psychoanalytic situation. Ideally, the psychoanalyst's interventions make it possible for the analysand to make discoveries about unconscious conflicts and their effects by making it easier and easier for him to say more and more of what is—with ever-increasing clarity and freedom from distortion—experienced by him as already "on his mind."

This description is meant to dissipate the impression sometimes given in writings by philosophers of science about psychoanalysis that "interpretations" in psychoanalysis are something like "you have an oedipal complex/castration anxiety/unconscious homosexual impulses." It is in fact here, with respect to the details about what is actually said by the psychoanalyst, using exactly what data, and with what actual response by the analysand, that the literature of psychoanalysis is especially (although considering problems of confidentiality somewhat understandably) lacking, and the literature of the philosophy of science (again, considering problems of access to such information, somewhat understandably) most misleading. An intervention by the psychoanalyst is frequently of the sort, "You seem to have some difficulty here, and I notice you have not said anything about what happened (just now/in yesterday's session), although we know in the past you have had strong feelings about that kind of thing." And the response of the analysand is frequently something like, "Oh yes, I was thinking about that when I came in, but forgot it by the time I got to the couch."

An interpretation, properly speaking, is an inference or hypothesis

---

1. For such an account of psychoanalytic technique, see, for example, Searl (1936).

about the analysand (not necessarily a psychoanalytic hypothesis) which follows logically or with some degree of probability from what the analysand has (or has not) said in conjunction with a general and perhaps probabilistic psychoanalytic hypothesis. Moreover, an interpretation usually is an inference or hypothesis which follows from more than one such conjunction. That is, one general psychoanalytic hypothesis in conjunction with what the analysand has said, and another general psychoanalytic hypothesis (independent of the first) in conjunction with other things the analysand has said, and so on, all entail a particular inference or hypothesis about the analysand—all entail the same interpretation. Glymour (1980) has explicated this kind of relation between hypothesis and evidence in science.

The psychoanalyst, for example, following a passing reference by the analysand to the relationship between psychoanalyst and analysand, may infer, by making use of general psychoanalytic hypotheses, that subsequent associations, although not manifestly about the relationship, are a disguised elaboration of this reference; or, following the occurrence of a significant event in the relationship, may infer, by making use of general psychoanalytic hypotheses, that subsequent associations, although not manifestly about the relationship, are a disguised account of how the analysand experienced this event (Gill and Hoffman, 1982). Such an inference does not necessarily or even most often involve "unconscious" contents, or contents which refer to long past events, but rather it may and ideally often does involve contents which have recently been in the analysand's awareness and are rather easily recalled by the analysand to awareness.

In addition to minimizing, by a disciplined use of psychoanalytic technique, suggesting to the analysand what to produce in his associations, which will then provide the basis for interpretations, the psychoanalyst must also be able to argue that suggestion does not determine the analysand's responses to an interpretation, especially if that response is to be taken at face value as both true and a "confirmation" of the psychoanalyst's inference. Such an inference or interpretation, to the extent it can be accepted as true, may be regarded in turn as providing evidential support for the set of different general psychoanalytic hypotheses from which, in conjunction with different reports of the analysand, it logically follows.

In some cases, it can be argued that there is no reason to suppose that what the analysand says is untrue, especially if it is a report about mental contents in the present or very recent past (and not an inference he is making from these contents or a possibly unreliable memory of contents in a more distant past).

In other cases, further productions or reports of the analysand follow from, and are predicted on the basis of, the interpretation or inference (perhaps in conjunction with some other general psychoanalytic hypothesis than the one from which, in conjunction with the analysand's reports, the inference was deduced in the first place). And just as sets of other reports in conjunction with other general psychoanalytic hypotheses may have led to or converged upon one particular inference or interpretation in the first place, so what the analysand reports or produces in response to the interpretation, in conjunction with some general psychoanalytic hypothesis (different from and independent of any psychoanalytic hypotheses used to deduce the interpretation), may also entail this same interpretation to which the analysand responds. These possibilities illustrate in part what is meant by the recommendation to rely on the production of new material by the analysand, rather than a "yes" or "no" response, in deciding whether the psychoanalyst's inference about the analysand is true.

Wisdom (1967) points out that the power of an interpretation to evoke a response can and should be distinguished from its truth. The only way to do so, he suggests, is for the investigator to predict what the analysand's response should be, or will be with some degree of probability, if the interpretation is to be provisionally accepted as true. Here, the interpretation or inference about the analysand, in conjunction with a general psychoanalytic hypothesis (different from and independent of any psychoanalytic hypothesis used to arrive at the interpretation), entails a given response or member of a finite class of responses from the analysand. What the psychoanalyst predicts will be the response to an interpretation clearly should not be merely an aspect of what has been previously manifested by the analysand and interpreted. For example, he may predict not only that an inferred motive will be preserved (and presumably become more explicit) in the analysand's response to an interpretation, but also that a particular defense, neither previously manifested nor suggested, will be apparent in the response.[2]

In addition to such efforts to reduce suggestion, the phenomenon of suggestion itself may be studied, and the extent of its influence measured. Edelson (1975) proposes investigation of the "causes" in the psy-

---

2. For other discussions relevant to a consideration of the question of using an analysand's response to an interpretation (aside from any therapeutic effect it may have) to de-

choanalytic situation of interpretation itself, by examining, for example, the linguistic features of the contexts (in Luborsky's sense) in which acts of interpretation occur. Similarly, such contexts may be examined to test hypotheses that the psychoanalyst responds to some contexts and ignores others when he speaks, is silent, or emits various kinds of verbal and nonverbal cues. Data can also be obtained to test, with respect to a particular phenomenon under investigation, just how plausible the hypothesis is that suggestion explains the productions of the analysand or his response to interpretations.

It also may be possible in seeking probative data in the psychoanalytic situation to try to select for observation relatively suggestion-resistant performances of the analysand. These performances may not involve or perhaps do not even permit focal awareness—for example, the analysand's choice of syntactic structures in his speech (Edelson, 1975). These performances, insofar as they are relatively immune to the psychoanalyst's influence and to the analysand's own preconceptions, may provide the psychoanalytic investigator with probative data. (Whether such data will measure variables of interest to the psychoanalyst is another question, but not one to be dismissively prejudged.)

Finally, it should be noted that philosophers of science tend to focus, for example, on the recovery of memories in psychoanalysis and the fallibility of such evidence, and to be unaware of or to ignore the kind of evidence obtained in the psychoanalytic situation as symptoms subside or disappear and are replaced by the transference neurosis. The essential characteristic of the transference neurosis—indeed what makes it possible for the analysand, assisted by the interpretations of the psychoanalyst, ultimately to achieve insight into its nature—is just precisely that neither its manifestations nor their intensity, neither the emerging wishes nor the fears of the analysand directed to the psychoanalyst, can be justified or explained merely or solely in terms of the ordinary conscious mental life of the analysand, the observable properties of the psychoanalyst, or the present objective reality of, or anything that actually occurs in, the psychoanalytic situation, however much features of that situation may serve as occasions for the emergence of such wishes or fears.

---

cide whether it should be accepted as true, see the volume edited by Paul (1963a) on psychoanalytic clinical interpretation, which includes especially relevant papers by Strachey (1934), Fenichel (1935), Freud (1937), Ezriel (1956, 1957), Wisdom (1956), Loewenstein (1957), and Paul (1963b). Also, see A. Kris (1982) and E. Kris (1956a, 1956b).

### 3. The Selection Bias of the Psychoanalyst and the Analysand's Preconceptions

The putative selection bias of the psychoanalyst is also subject to empirical study. How does in fact a focal theme or focal conflict (Luborsky and Mintz, 1974), dominating one session after another, emerge from a period of apparently "chaotic" associations? Is it really at the prompting of the psychoanalyst?

What Grünbaum suggests is certainly not true—that the psychoanalyst has no prior criteria for selecting among associations. He can distinguish between, and give different weight to the contents associated with, different types of "free" association. He observes the degree to which "free" association is deliberately or unwittingly monitored and organized by the analysand, or instead flows relatively unimpeded by tendentious selectiveness, censorial judgments, or conscious purposiveness.

Indeed, it should not be supposed that it is always necessary for the psychoanalyst to *infer* the analysand's unconscious wishes, thoughts, or fantasies. These progressively emerge into consciousness, often with an astonishing explicitness and degree of convincing mundane detail, as conscious purposiveness is temporarily abandoned or suspended in the psychoanalytic situation.[3] Here, in observing variations in the quality of free association itself, the psychoanalyst is able to separate data "contaminated" by one kind of influence (the patient's selectiveness) from data relatively uncontaminated by that kind of influence.[4]

Furthermore, I think Grünbaum may be incorrect when he implies that the psychoanalyst justifies his inferences from free association by appealing to the "causal role of repression" in neurosis (on the model of the case of Anna O.), a role which, of course, Grünbaum is at some pains to show has not been established. What appears to me to be presupposed instead by the method of free association (in the same sense

3. Grünbaum is correct, of course, in pointing out that the existence of such wishes, thoughts, or fantasies is not by itself sufficient to justify conclusions about their causal role or relevance, however plausible or irresistible such conclusions may seem. That, however, poses no impossible difficulty. Deducing and demonstrating covariations are, of course, the minimal next steps.

4. Interest in obtaining "free associations" to an item, in order to explain that item, has given way to interest in what accounts for the vicissitudes of free association itself, especially interest in what kinds of difficulties the analysand has in reporting what is on his mind and what accounts for these difficulties (Searl, 1936; A. Kris, 1982).

that laws of physics are presupposed in the use of a microscope or telescope), as far as Freud was concerned, is that mental processes are purposive. I take it that this presupposition is equivalent to the assertions that, first, all mental processes are related or oriented to, serve, or are governed, caused, or produced by purposes and, second, therefore, that one particular content follows another itself is directly or indirectly determined by the purpose(s) governing a stream of associations. Freud mentions two additional theorems, apparently presupposed as well, which he claims provide the rationale for his method. The two theorems, which he calls the "basic pillars" of psychoanalytic technique, are "that, when conscious purposive ideas are abandoned, concealed purposive ideas assume control of the current of ideas, and that superficial associations are only substitutes by displacement for suppressed deeper ones" (1900, p. 531).

If I am correct in assuming that these theorems are presupposed by the method of free association, then that method cannot, of course, be used to provide evidential support for them. Freud frequently appealed to the existence of independent evidence for what the method presupposes to be true. The phenomena of hypnosis are important to him, perhaps for this reason. In a 1909 footnote he claims that the two theorems have "been experimentally employed and confirmed by Jung and his pupils in their studies in word-association" (1900, pp. 531–532). It perhaps goes without saying that psychoanalysts should make explicit—following careful logical analysis—what assumptions about the mind are presupposed by the method of free association, and should accept the responsibility to obtain evidential support for these assumptions independently of this method that presupposes their truth.

The psychoanalyst is also especially alert to the analysand's biases in perceiving and organizing experience. Wherever experience is ambiguous, the analysand interprets it in a particular way. For example, he attributes motives, thoughts, and feelings to others, and highlights one aspect of a situation while casting another aspect in shadow. It does not make sense (here "does not make sense" is equivalent to "is improbable") that all ambiguous experiences should be given the same "reading," endowed with the same features—that is, that reality-accommodated interpretations would resolve ambiguity over and over in the same way. Since it does not make sense, it calls for psychoanalytic explanation.

Ambiguity, and stereotypy in the analysand's resolution of ambiguity, are important prior criteria for what the psychoanalyst selects to attend and respond to, on the hypothesis that such stereotypy may be an outcome of unconscious conflict and, specifically, of the analysand's greater propensity, in an ambiguous situation, to perceive opportunities for gratification of unconscious wishes, to ferret out obstacles to that gratification, and to resolve ambiguity in the direction of wish-fulfillment. These criteria underlie the technical importance of attention to transference phenomena and of "working through." It should not be difficult to make other prior criteria of selection, in Grünbaum's sense, explicit, and to examine to what extent in a particular study the psychoanalyst is governed by or departs from them.

In general, the psychoanalyst is a clinical instrument with many unknown and some remarkable properties. His properties, capacities, and performances need to be investigated—for example, the preconscious processes making it possible for him to conjoin different psychoanalytic hypotheses he knows and different data in the psychoanalytic situation to which he is exposed and of which he wittingly or unwittingly takes note; to arrive at inferences about the analysand from such conjunctions; to match these inferences about the analysand with each other and with subsequent inferences; and to decide when and how to convey such inferences in interpretations to the analysand, where the "when" and "how" of an act of interpretation and not only its content determine whether or not it will lead to the achievement of veridical insight by the analysand. The psychoanalyst's ability to detect, accept, and reflect upon small signs or signals of his own internal and regulated reciprocations of, or empathic identifications with, more or less covert wishes and fears of the analysand (which in the psychoanalytic situation have reawakened and intensified in the transference) is surely important here. Manifestations of this ability, of course, belong to the context of discovery (generating hypotheses) and not to the context of justification (testing hypotheses).

Finally, with regard to the influence of the analysand's preconceptions about himself (which are not necessarily independent of psychoanalytic theory), as well as the influence of the psychoanalyst's suggestions and selection bias, I should wonder about a factor neglected in most writing about psychoanalysis by philosophers of science. It is neither general explanations nor obvious positive instances of psychoanalytic hypotheses that appear to be especially important to either psychoanalyst or analysand. Rather, what is given special weight by both is the emergence of circumstantial detail, having an astonishing degree of specificity and idiosyncratic nuance, in reports of fantasies and interpretations of experience. Such details have not previously been remembered by the analysand (or at least have not been an object of his focal awareness or conscious reflection) and almost certainly have not previously been imagined or guessed in advance by the psychoanalyst. A psychoanalysis without surprises cannot properly be termed a psychoanalysis at all. One cannot regard as plausible that such data have been suggested in any ordinary sense of that word. It is these data that may in the end prove to be most relevant to the search in the psychoanalytic situation for probative evidence providing support for psychoanalytic hypotheses.

## 4. The Fallibility of Memory

In general, I believe that Grünbaum's justifiable emphasis on the fallibility of memory does tend to underestimate the autonomous functioning of memory—that aspect of memory which, in Piaget's sense, is accommodative—and the possibility of detecting which aspects of memory are the results of accommodation to reality as it is and which are the outcome of distortion or fictive construction, as a result of unconscious conflicts involving wish-fulfillment and defense. Psychoanalysts often feel that they can intuitively distinguish between effects of what "really happened to the analysand"—when an outcome is an adjustment to a noxious reality—and effects of what the analysand imagined, where "what happened" was merely used as material in his imagining. It is possible that making explicit the criteria by which one separates one aspect of a memory from another—appealing no doubt to general knowledge of what is possible and impossible, as well as to internal evidence converging on one conclusion rather than others in the mass of associations—would prove a fruitful avenue of investigation, both theoretically and methodologically. Spence (1982) is especially and I believe unduly pessimistic about solving this problem. His pessimism leads him to despair over the possibility of, and to abandon the quest for, general objective truth in the psychoanalytic situation. It is premature to give up in that situation on Freud's attempt to approximate the unknown reality—and to turn instead, as Spence has apparently done, to a hermeneutic pursuit of a satisfying, coherent, and nongeneralizable "reading" of a singular case.

# 10    How Might Achievement of the Objectives of Psychoanalytic Treatment Be Assessed?

Grünbaum's discussion of the tally argument deserves special attention. It would be easy to reply to him, cavalierly, that there is no simple relation between theoretical knowledge and practical achievements. The truth of scientific hypotheses does not necessarily entail as a consequence the success of technological enterprises (such as therapy) in which these hypotheses are applied. Grünbaum knows this (1977a, pp. 220–221). The failure to demonstrate that psychoanalytic therapy is efficacious may have any number of explanations, which are consistent with the truth of psychoanalytic hypotheses. It is also conceivable that psychoanalytic therapy might be demonstrated to be efficacious, even though psychoanalytic hypotheses are false.

## 1. Psychoanalysis as Treatment and the Achievement of Veridical Insight

However, it is difficult to escape the conclusion that what is distinctive about psychoanalysis as treatment must surely be the shared quest by psychoanalyst and analysand for what is true about the analysand, about the particulars of his psychic reality (his acts of imagination), and also the particulars of the actual world in which he lives and has lived, and about how he has acted upon this world, how he has been acted upon by it, and what use he has made of it as material in producing psychological entities and structures.

The operative word is truth. Psychoanalyst and analysand seek accounts which—whether plausible, meaningful, satisfying, and coherent, or eccentric, meaningless, painful, and chaotic—can be accepted provisionally as closer and closer approximations to what is *true* of the analysand. The account sought is an account that corresponds to what the analysand is (and "what he is" includes his mental life, his fantasies, his wishes, and his propensities to interpret ambiguous experience one way rather than another). The analysand and his subjectivity are part of the world as it is, the same world which in another aspect is outside him, upon which he acts and which acts upon him. It is this actual world in both its internal (subjective) and external aspects—and not any possible world at all, however gratifying, plausible, or meaningful that possible world might be—that the psychoanalyst and analysand seek to know.

A psychoanalysis that does not seek an increase in veridical knowledge of self, that might be considered successful although a change in the accuracy of representation of and attitudes toward oneself and the world in which one lives is no part of its outcome, is a contradiction in terms.

The psychoanalyst wishes to make use of psychoanalytic hypotheses that he has some justification for provisionally accepting as true (in the "corresponding-to-the-actual-world" sense of "true") and which he intends to put to the test every time he makes an interpretation. For his aim, in the spirit of Freud's commitment to truth, is to enable the analysand to acquire veridical insight. The claim of psychoanalysis to distinctiveness as a treatment in my view depends upon the claim that the acquisition of veridical insight by the analysand is a necessary condition, although probably not a sufficient condition, for the efficacy of this treatment.

## 2. The Objectives of Psychoanalysis as Treatment

When we say efficacy, we allude to outcomes sought by psychoanalysis. Veridical insight is necessary, even if not sufficient, to bring about just these outcomes. What are they?

The problems involved in investigating the outcomes of psychoanalysis as treatment are vexing, but I do not believe that comparing with methodological rigor different treatment modalities according to their ability to achieve goals sought by some and not by others is any solution to these problems. For example, mitigation of symptoms in and of itself by any means is not a primary or distinctive objective of psychoanalytic treatment, but that is not to say that psychoanalysts have been especially helpful in making explicit what its primary and distinctive objectives are.

The following outcomes surely cannot be included among the primary, distinctive objectives of psychoanalytic treatment:

*a*) temporary remission of symptoms, whether due to suggestion or favorable life circumstances;

*b*) a mere inadvertent strengthening of (pathogenic) defenses or substituting of one (pathogenic) defense for another; or even;

*c*) long-lasting alleviation of illness, when such alleviation depends upon continued exposure of the analysand to life circumstances so favorable they preclude recurrence of what previously instigated pathological formations.

The following statements, however, do express what probably should be included among the primary, distinctive objectives of such treatment.

*a*) Psychoanalysis aims to bring about not only a mitigation of symptoms but a permanent decrease in the patient's propensity to respond with symptom-formation to the *same* kinds and degrees of frustration and deprivation that before treatment resulted in regression and symptom-formation. Given Freud's postulation of a complementary series, which requires always assessing the relative contribution of both experience and constitution, and his postulation of constitutional predispositions or propensities to fixation and conflict in the genesis of neurosis, psychoanalysis cannot claim that, following therapy, *no* circumstances, *no* kind or degree of frustration or deprivation, will ever result in symptom-formation. Psychoanalytic therapy cannot claim to mitigate constitutional pathogenic dispositions, nor can it claim that the patient's improved capacity to manage frustration, deprivation, or conflict without resort to symptom-formation is adequate to *any* degree of challenge, no matter how severe. However, should symptom-formation occur following a successful outcome of psychoanalytic therapy, one might expect that the analysand will achieve veridical insight with or without help more rapidly than before, and that, whatever symptoms occur, they will be less severe and more short-lived than before.

Clearly, there is no guarantee that an analysand will end up pleased or happy with himself, others, or the world he lives in—only that his discontent and misery are now determined by intransigent obstacles in the world impinging upon him, and by the unavoidable chasm yawning between his wish and his power to gratify it—and not by unconscious fantasies or conflicts.

*b*) Psychoanalysis aims to bring about de-automatization of automatisms—automatic reactions, where one might expect reflection and choice. Not the least of such automatisms is the propensity to interpret experience, to the extent it is ambiguous, according to unconscious fantasies. Externalizations (interpreting another's actions, or attributing to another motives or attitudes in relation to oneself, without awareness that one's own characteristics serve as the model) and internalizations (acting toward oneself, or adopting motives or attitudes in relation to oneself, or viewing oneself in a particular way, without awareness that the characteristics of another serve as the model) provide—in unconscious and distorted attempts at wish-fulfillment—ways of interpreting experience so that it conforms or alludes in a disguised form to unconscious fantasies. Therefore, because these fantasies are unconscious and result in wish-fulfillment, not gratification, the analysand's interpretations of experience are peremptory, automatic, stereotypic, and repeated over and over; ambiguities are resolved in different contexts and on different occasions in the same way, regardless of the consequences.

Veridical insights both diminish, and result from diminishing, motivational impediments to accommodative aspects of perception and memory, especially when these motivational impediments involve distortive transformations. Veridical insights eventually lead to changes in the analysand's attitudes toward (interpretations and appraisals of) himself, significant figures in his life, and the vicissitudes of his life—as well as expand the range of interpretations and appraisals he brings to bear in responding to experience. However, if (and to the extent) changes are inspired by *false* "insights" or pseudoinsights, then maladaptive action, inappropriate appraisals, distorted or stereotyped interpretations of experience, and symptom-formation are more likely to continue or recur than not.

Veridical insight both causes and follows relaxation of automatic constraints upon psychological functioning, and diminution of the extent to which—and the number of contexts in which—psychological functioning proceeds in an automatic way to a predetermined end. As such changes occur, the analysand's interest, and the pleasure he takes, in his own mental processes (imagining, thinking, feeling), regardless of their content, increase. This emphasis on the mitigation of automatic responses to experience does not, of course, call into question that some automatisms have adaptive value (Hartmann, 1958).

The content or direction of changes in the analysand's attitudes is not specified in stating objectives of psychoanalytic treatment, for surely this content depends in part at least on what the analysand's veridical insights are; the psychoanalyst can have no foreknowledge of what these insights will be. The analysand's application of veridical insights acquired in psychoanalysis to his life also is not automatically predetermined by therapy; it is up to him, a matter of reflection and choice. He has acquired tools, but no a priori prescription exists telling him whether, when, or how to use them. He is free to attend to or ignore such insights, to change or not this or that about himself on the basis of such insights, to change in one way rather than another. So long as he possesses adequate knowledge and is able to reflect, what choices the patient actually makes should not affect any judgment about the success or failure of treatment.

*c*) The analysand's decreased propensity to form symptoms, decreased sphere of automaticity, and altered and expanded set of interpretations and appraisals of himself and his world may contribute to an enhanced capacity *both* to love and to work, although here too whether and how the analysand chooses, reflecting on veridical insights, to manifest this enhanced capacity in the varied circumstances in which he finds himself should not affect any judgment about the success or failure of treatment.

## 3. Some Tasks Facing Psychoanalysis

What is striking about these objectives is that they involve changes in the analysand's propensities or dispositions, and not necessarily changes in how these are displayed; they do not stipulate unequivocal and unique changes in his manifest behavior. A methodological task facing psychoanalysis, then, is to devise means of detecting and demonstrating alterations in such propensities or dispositions.

My guess is that it is first of all in the psychoanalytic situation itself that the psychoanalyst may be able to identify the condition or contexts in which such dispositions manifest themselves, and to detect changes in these dispositions throughout the process of the psychoanalytic treatment itself. Clearly, he must find a way to measure these dispositions and changes in their strength, for example, by observing and measuring changes in the way in which the analysand attempts in this situation to convey in free association without judgment or selection everything on his mind; changes in the way the analysand in this situation resolves ambiguities; and exacerbations and mitigations of the analysand's symptoms.

An additional task facing psychoanalysis is to specify not only what properties in addition to truth an interpretation must have for veridical insight to result, but what in addition to the acquisition of veridical insight is necessary for these desired objectives to be achieved. Interpretation in and of itself, insight in and of itself, even though veridical, even though necessary, do not seem to be sufficient. Otherwise, psychoanalysis might be better deemed, rather than therapy, a purely cognitive educational intervention, which achieves its effects through the transmission by an "instructor" of knowledge to a "student."

One need neither underestimate the difficulties of carrying out such tasks, nor on the other hand abandon them. In any event, the goal of obtaining evidential support for the hypothesis that such objectives as these are more likely to be achieved by means of psychoanalytic treatment than by means of no treatment, or by means of any other treatment (if there be any such treatment) purporting to achieve the *same* objectives without recourse to interpretation or the acquisition of veridical insight by the patient, is not to be despised.

Grünbaum is not convincing when he argues that there is no evidence to show that psychoanalytic interpretations are necessary to achieve a successful outcome of psychoanalytic theory, because (so he says) the *same* kind of outcome (this is the hooker) has been shown to result from life events and the interventions of rival therapies. I do agree with him, however, that it is the responsibility of psychoanalysis, not of its challengers, to obtain evidence that supports the claim that psychoanalytic treatment is efficacious. I do not believe, however, that testing psychoanalytic hypotheses in the psychoanalytic situation must wait achievement of this goal.

# 11     Psychoanalytic Hypotheses Can Be and Have Been Tested in the Psychoanalytic Situation

The existence of at least two counterexamples refutes or at least casts strong doubt upon Grünbaum's generalization that it is in principle impossible to test psychoanalytic hypotheses in the psychoanalytic situation. One counterexample is supplied by Luborsky's invention of a symptom-context method for obtaining quantitative probative data in the psychoanalytic situation to test psychoanalytic hypotheses according to the canons of eliminative inductivism (1967, 1973), and his use of this method in single subject research (Luborsky and Mintz, 1974). Luborsky devised a matched-samples design to satisfy the requirement that a comparison between at least two conditions be included in describing an effect or outcome of interest—a requirement the importance of which Grünbaum so emphasizes and which he apparently regards as impossible to meet in the psychoanalytic situation.

The second counterexample is supplied by Glymour's explication of a so-called bootstrap strategy in testing scientific theories (viewed as sets of multiple interrelated but independent hypotheses), which he believes is characteristic of actual scientific practice—and as much exemplified by Freud's Rat Man case study as, for example, by Newton's way of testing the laws of particle mechanics (Glymour, 1974, 1980).

## 1. The Case of Miss X

For various reasons, Luborsky and Mintz (1974) do not present their study clearly as a test of a psychoanalytic hypothesis. (As is evident in Luborsky's 1967 paper, he is excited most by the aspect of his work that is in the context of discovery.) However, they certainly could have chosen to do so, and I shall formulate the argument about hypothesis and evidence in the study as they might have formulated it, if they had chosen to present the study as that kind of test.

Here, then, is the argument about the relation between hypothesis and evidence in this study, stated in terms that will make clear how and to what extent the study satisfies the canons of eliminate inductivism.

**144**

*a*) Miss X, a psychological domain, is a Freudian system. [Theoretical hypothesis.][1]

*b*) Miss X manifests thirteen instances of momentary forgetting in around three hundred sessions of psychoanalysis. [Phenomena of interest—variations in presence and absence of momentary forgetting.]

*c*) An increase in the intensity of a focal conflict is necessary to cause the appearance of neurotic symptoms or parapraxes, or to cause an aggravation of their severity. [This hypothesis follows from *a*, and from the definition of the theoretical predicate " . . . is a Freudian system," and must be satisfied by the domain Miss X if *a* is to be provisionally accepted as true.]

*d*) An instance of momentary forgetting is an instance of a neurotic symptom or parapraxis. [Follows from a characterization of momentary forgetting as meeting definitional criteria for "neurotic symptom" or "parapraxis."]

*e*) If Miss X is emotionally involved with her psychoanalyst, a focal conflict is intensified. [Follows from psychoanalytic hypotheses about transference phenomena and the development of a transference neurosis in the psychoanalytic situation.]

*f*) Miss X's propensity, on an occasion she suffers an episode of momentary forgetting, to be emotionally involved with her psychoanalyst is stronger than it is on some occasion she suffers no such episode of momentary forgetting. In other words, the degree of emotional involvement of Miss X with her psychoanalyst is much greater in those contexts in which momentary forgetting occurs than it is in those contexts in which momentary forgetting does not occur. [This is the predicted outcome of the study, stated probabilistically. It follows from *c*, *d*, and *e*.]

*g*) A context is a passage from a psychoanalytic session of a certain length preceding and following the occurrence of a symptom. A control context is a matched passage, of similar length and the same amount of time into the session, from a nearly contiguous session in which no symptom occurred. In an ideal execution of this research design, all

---

1. My use here of a theoretical hypothesis which asserts that a theoretical predicate is true of a single subject regarded as a domain follows from my previous discussion in Chapter 6 of psychoanalytic theory in the framework of the nonstatement view of theory. It is not essential to the argument that this study tests a psychoanalytic hypothesis in the psychoanalytic situation, and that the test satisfies the requirements Grünbaum insists such a test must meet.

contexts would be scored blindly for emotional involvement with the psychoanalyst (not just any kind of emotion) by judges who do not know in which contexts the symptom occurred; thus the possibility that the bias of judges explains the outcome is excluded.

*h*) Each pair of contexts, different with respect to whether momentary forgetting has or has not occurred, has been matched (with respect to the temporal proximity of sessions and the temporal location of passages in the sessions), so that the contexts can otherwise in crucial respects be regarded as equivalent. Such matching is intended to exclude the possibility that some other difference between the contexts accounts for the fact that momentary forgetting occurs more frequently in association with one kind of context than the other. The contexts are matched by a method (using automatic criteria) which excludes the influence of a selection bias as accounting for the outcome.

*i*) The predicted outcome is observed. The null hypothesis that the outcome might be expected to occur by extraneous influences alone, acting randomly (not all in one direction), even in the absence of any relation between emotional involvement with the psychoanalyst (resulting in intensification of conflict) and momentary forgetting, is eliminated by statistical test. That is, the particular outcome observed would be much rarer if the null hypothesis were true than if the hypothesis being tested were true, and therefore the outcome tends to support the latter rather than the former.

It is important to note the rarity of the phenomenon (thirteen instances of momentary forgetting in something like three hundred sessions), which in itself tends to eliminate unwitting suggestion by the psychoanalyst (arising from his interest in the phenomenon) as a cause of its appearance. It is even more difficult to see how suggestion, or the preconceptions or expectations of the analysand, could play a role in ensuring that instances of momentary forgetting occur more frequently in relation to certain contexts than others, and that, in the kind of contexts in which they do tend to occur, they do so not invariably but in fact relatively rarely. (This latter fact is, of course, consistent with the hypothesis that the intensification of conflict is, put nonprobabilistically, a necessary but not a sufficient condition for the occurrence of a symptom or parapraxis.)

It is true, of course, that the relation between intensification of conflict and momentary forgetting is a statistical association. No evidence has been obtained which supports the hypothesis that this relation is also causal. However, while it does not follow from the fact that a relation is a statistical association that it is also causal, the reverse is not the case. That a relation between two variables is causal does entail that there is a statistical relation between them. Therefore, the study tests the causal hypothesis. For, if the evidence did not support that a statistical relation holds between the variables, the hypothesis that a causal relation holds between them is falsified.

Therefore, in turn, the hypothesis that the domain Miss X is a Freudian system did in this study stand in risk of being falsified, whether other domains (other single subjects) are Freudian systems or not. The risk was considerable, since the investigator has no warrant from background knowledge or any other theory for believing that the phenomenon momentary forgetting depends in any way or in this way upon the degree of Miss X's emotional involvement with her psychoanalyst (not just any increase in emotion).

I do not, of course, claim that the study is a perfect one, regarded, for example, from the point of view of the canons of eliminative inductivism. There are, no doubt, methodological problems here.[2] However, there is no reason to dismiss it as an achievement that successfully casts considerable doubt on Grünbaum's conclusion.

## 2. The Case of the Rat Man

Glymour (1980) holds a theory to be a set of interrelated but independent hypotheses.[3] He rejects the hypothetico-deductive model of testing a theory in toto by deducing an empirical consequence from it. Instead, he regards scientists such as Newton—also, Freud using the existence or nonexistence of states of affairs as data in the Rat Man case, and social scientists using nonexperimental data and the strategy of causal modeling—to be testing *subsets* of the interrelated but independent hypotheses of a theory through a kind of bootstrap strategy. This strategy makes it possible to reject and revise a subset of hypotheses without abandoning an entire theory. The bootstrap strategy, prototypically, matches a prediction made from the conjunction of at least one fact and one hypothesis with a prediction made from the conjunction of at least one other fact and the same or another hypothesis.[4]

The form of relations between or among different variables in a

2. I shall discuss this study and Luborsky's important methodological innovation more systematically, more critically, and in greater detail in *Single Subject Research*.

3. Hypotheses are interrelated if they make use of at least one variable in common, and are independent if they are not deducible from each other.

4. See technical note 5.

theory is stated by each hypothesis that is part of the theory. Some of the variables of a theory are nontheoretical. Their values are obtained by making empirical observations, carrying out operations, or taking measurements. Some of the variables of a theory are theoretical. The value of a theoretical variable is obtained by calculating it, using a law or hypothesis and the value assigned to another variable (nontheoretical or theoretical) to which the theoretical variable is related by some function.

According to the bootstrap strategy, IF:

*a*) the hypotheses in a set of hypotheses about a domain are interrelated (the hypotheses have one or more than one variable in common), but independent (no one hypothesis is entailed by any other);

*b*) and one of the hypotheses, together with a set of observation statements, entails a statement;

*c*) and the statement that is entailed by this hypothesis and set of observation statements is also entailed by a second hypothesis in conjunction with another set of observation statements, or the statement entailed by this hypothesis and set of observation statements is also an instance of (entailed by) the second hypothesis;

*d*) and this result occurs repeatedly, as one compares what is entailed by the same hypothesis and different sets of observation statements, or what is entailed by different hypotheses each with different sets of observation statements;

THEN it is justifiable to accept provisionally as true a *conjunction* of just those hypotheses so tested.

A competition between rival theories is decided by referring to a complicated set of criteria, including: the number of independent hypotheses in each which have survived such tests, the extent to which hypotheses in each have survived multiple tests, and the extent to which hypotheses in each which have survived such tests are central rather than peripheral.

In the Rat Man case, the variables are states of affairs, and their values are not quantities but the classificatory or categorical values "exists" and "does not exist."

The patient's report of conscious guilt over his father's death in conjunction with a psychoanalytic hypothesis stated by Freud entails the interpretation that there exists an unconscious thought for which guilt is appropriate. The patient's report of the fears he felt at the conscious thought of his father's death in conjunction with another independent psychoanalytic hypothesis stated by Freud entails the interpretation that the patient unconsciously wished for his father's death. But this conclusion in turn entails the *same* state of affairs entailed by the other fact and hypothesis—the existence of an unconscious thought for which guilt is appropriate.

In turn, the unconscious wish for the father's death in conjunction with another psychoanalytic hypothesis entails an infantile conscious wish for the father's death. This state of affairs in conjunction with another psychoanalytic hypothesis entails an infantile conflict with the father over sensual desires. This state of affairs in conjunction with another psychoanalytic hypothesis entails that such a conflict with the father occurred before the age of six. This state of affairs in conjunction with another psychoanalytic hypothesis entails that, before the age of six, the patient was punished by the father for masturbating.

According to Glymour, since this last prediction was disconfirmed, Freud chose to revise the set of hypotheses by rejecting the hypothesis that called for such an actual event. He added instead a hypothesis about the causal role of fantasy or psychic reality.

Grünbaum seems to accept the validity of Glymour's strategy; he certainly does not argue that it violates the canons of eliminative inductivism. At the same time, Grünbaum dismisses the particular application of the strategy to Freud's Rat Man case study. His argument that the data here are contaminated ignores Glymour's basis for regarding as reasonable the selection of the analysand's reports of certain conscious thoughts and feelings as nontheoretical facts, since these do not require knowledge of psychoanalytic hypotheses to obtain or to evaluate as true or false.

Grünbaum also chooses to regard the appeal in this case to extraclinical data (historical information)—required to confirm the particular set of hypotheses here being tested—as somehow inevitable in any use of the bootstrap strategy to test psychoanalytic hypotheses with data obtained in the psychoanalytic situation. Such tests, he concludes, will always be parasitic on extraclinically obtained data; Glymour's analysis of Freud's reasoning in this case, then, actually supports the conclusion that psychoanalytic hypotheses cannot be tested with data obtained *solely* in the psychoanalytic situation.

However, there is nothing in Glymour's explication of his strategy or analysis of its use in the Rat Man case to suggest that reliance on extraclinical data is necessarily required by this strategy or this kind of use of it. Surely, the need for extraclinical nontheoretical facts in any instance will depend on which particular hypotheses are tested (they need not, for example, be etiologic hypotheses or concerned with the genesis of a neurosis in the distant past), and whether what nontheoretical facts are needed in any instance are in fact available in the psychoanalytic situation itself.

Ultimately, Grünbaum rejects the use of Glymour's method in the clinical situation, not because clinical data are contaminated, but because even if they were not contaminated, and even if the patient had remembered being punished before age six by the father for masturbating, and even if this memory were accepted as veridical, there is no way, he claims, to use such data to support a hypothesis that this remote event is causally relevant to the development of the patient's neurosis.

In responding to Grünbaum, I shall leave aside the question of the probative value in testing causal hypotheses of predicting from a set of such hypotheses that an event had occurred, which prior to the prediction was not known to have occurred, and the occurrence of which would not have been predicted on the basis of background knowledge alone without the set of hypotheses. (Prediction and postdiction are here logically equivalent.) There is, in any case, some question whether this particular event could be regarded as improbable or unexpected in the sense required.

However, Grünbaum asserts the impossibility of supporting with clinical data a hypothesis about the causal relevance of a pathogenic agent that is an event remote in time from the phenomena actually available for study. It is the "pastness," the remoteness, of the event that is at issue for Grünbaum. In the Anna O. case, the pathogenic agent (repression of an event) was relatively recent, recovery of the memory of the event had a therapeutic effect, and the method of recovery was independently applied to and effective with separate symptoms. If therapeutic effects had been reliably achieved, then Grünbaum might not have asserted that the use of clinical data to support a hypothesis about the causal relevance of a putative pathogen to symptom-formation is impossible, or at least he might have qualified this assertion in important ways.

But, in fact, in psychoanalysis the pathogen is not merely a remote event, or a series of such events, the effect of which lives on. The pathogen reappears in all its virulence, with increasing frankness and explicitness, in the transference—in a new edition, a new version, a reemergence, a repetition of the past pathogenic events or factors. Even from the point of view of treatment, as Freud pointed out, it is not possible to hang a pathogen in effigy. A radical cure, as distinct from melioration of terminal consequences, is intended to attack the pathogen directly, and if it is to be attacked it must be present.

In this connection, Fenichel (1941, pp. 42–43, 49) points out that the patient's childhood "is still actively present . . . in the behavior of the patient today; otherwise it would not interest us at all." He recommends that interpretations, which seek to reverse "displacements," abolish "isolations," or guide "traces of affect to their proper relationships," concern themselves with the play of impulse and defense in the tranference. "If only we put the present in order correctly and understand it, we shall thereby make new impulses possible for the patient, until the childhood material comes of itself."

The pathogen together with its pathological effects are, therefore, under the investigator's eye, so to speak, in the psychoanalytic situation, and demonstrating the causal relation between them in that situation, by nonexperimental or quasi-experimental methods, surely provides support, even if indirect, for the hypothesis that in the past the same kind of pathogenic factors were necessary to bring about the same kind of effects.

Transference interpretations, not just any kind of interpretations, may constitute the mutative interventions, not only in traditional psychoanalysis (see, e.g., Gill, 1982; Malan, 1979; and Strachey, 1934), but perhaps in brief psychoanalytic psychotherapy as well (Malan, 1976), where it is easier to study their overall efficacy. Furthermore, it is certainly possible to demonstrate the immediate therapeutic effects of such interventions using data from the clinical situation (Luborsky et al., 1979).

Grünbaum tends to ignore these possibilities, first, because the hypothesis he is concerned with is what he calls the "repression etiology" hypothesis, and, second, because he regards "transference" as denoting a contaminant of the relevant clinical data rather than as denoting the relevant clinical data themselves.

As a matter of fact, psychoanalysis does not hold repression to be the pathogen. Intrapsychic conflict, involving a variety of defenses, one of which may be repression, is a pathogen. Even if repression operates, it is as likely to be directed against awareness of the connection or relation between or among contents as against the awareness of contents themselves. These contents are not simply memories of the past that must be recovered, but current psychological events, in which impulses and defenses against them are activated and reactivated. The alternation of substitute-formations, such as symptoms, parapraxes, and dreams, with expressions of impulse and defense in the transference, is the process investigated by the psychoanalyst.

Grünbaum's attitude toward transference as a contaminant is a bit like the attitude of a generation of workers toward the clear areas on agar plates. For them, these clear areas indicated the presence of a contaminant, which had frustrated their efforts to culture bacteria for study. It took a creative refocus to see the putative contaminant as a potential therapeutic agent whose properties and effects should be studied. In the same way, Freud refocused on resistance phenomena in general and transference phenomena in particular.

In concluding this response to Grünbaum's evaluation of Glymour's application of his bootstrap method to clinical material, I suggest that not only is failure to pay sufficient attention to the centrality of transference an obstacle to the success of the psychoanalytic treatment enterprise, but an obstacle as well to the success of any attempt, using data from the psychoanalytic situation, to test psychoanalytic hypotheses.

In passing, I note that Glymour, holding to a view of theory as a set of interrelated but independent hypotheses, rejects the nonstatement view of theory, apparently because he regards it as implying that a theory must be tested in toto. The theoretical hypothesis tested in the nonstatement view is a claim that a theoretical predicate is true of a particular domain, irrespective of whether or not there are domains of which it is not true; the theoretical hypothesis is true of a domain if and only if all the members of a set of laws or interrelated but independent hypotheses are true in that domain. However, in testing such a theoretical hypothesis, one might easily use Glymour's bootstrap strategy to examine whether or not a set of interrelated but independent hypotheses is true of a domain. If these hypotheses together define the theoretical predicate, and one or more of them is disconfirmed by this strategy, then the theoretical hypothesis claiming the theoretical predicate is true of the domain must be rejected. Glymour's strategy, however, would then in fact be in addition ideally suited to revising the definition of a rejected theoretical predicate that has otherwise proved useful, by changing just some (disconfirmed) laws or hypotheses in a set of laws or hypotheses, rather than discarding the whole set and therefore the theoretical predicate altogether.

Such considerations lead me to think that a first attempt at making use of the nonstatement view of theory might place emphasis, in characterizing a theory, on the choice of the set of variables used in defining a theoretical predicate, rather than on the particular form that relations between or among these variables take. This is to propose that, in the social sciences at least, laws or hypotheses used in defining a theoretical predicate might not be required to specify functions and constants; rather, a domain might be considered a certain kind of system if and only if it were true that a specified set of variables descriptive of entities in the domain were related in some unspecified way. (This proposal is, of course, very far from the way Suppes and Stegmüller, for example, conceive of the nonstatement view of theory.) Achen (1982) argues, similarly, that good social science theories do *not* specify the exact form of relationships among variables. Herbst (1970), in discussing single subject research, also makes a similar point when he suggests that that a set of variables is related may be true across "behavioral worlds" (from one single subject to another), but how these variables are related (for example, linearly or nonlinearly) may vary from subject to subject, and what functions as a constant in a law or hypothesis true of one subject rarely, if ever, holds constant from subject to subject. Rozeboom (1961) comes at the matter from a different direction, when he supposes that variables are discovered through a process of induction in the course of empirical work; different types of variables (and, therefore, different concepts) emerge, for example, as what is a constant or parameter in a law or hypothesis at one level itself varies from setting to setting, from group to group, or from subject to subject, and thus becomes a variable in a "higher order" law or hypothesis.

Glymour provides psychoanalysis with one way of arguing the relation between hypothesis and evidence in a single case study—even though the study be both nonexperimental and nonquantitative. His strategy is an important contribution (whatever the imperfections in the argument or data in one or another study). Making use of it, instead of telling a "story" which mixes hypotheses and facts indiscriminately, is very likely to increase the cogency of scientific reasoning in psychoanalysis.

# Conclusion

# 12  A Research Program for a New Generation of Psychoanalytic Investigators

This work has been in the nature of a review and an assessment of the scientific status of psychoanalysis, especially in the light of new conceptions in the philosophy of science. Current threats to its scientific status arise especially from the following circumstances.

1. Reasoning about the relation of hypothesis and evidence in the case reports of psychoanalysis does not satisfy the canons of eliminative inductivism. On the whole, it cannot convince another, not necessarily a psychoanalyst, who is both rational and skeptical, that the evidence the psychoanalytic investigator presents does indeed justify provisionally accepting as true the hypothesis the investigator claims is more credible scientifically than another rival or alternative hypothesis.

2. Many psychoanalysts feel increasingly unable—and therefore that it is futile or untenable—to argue that, from the psychoanalytic situation, data can be obtained which will provide evidential support, according to scientific canons, for psychoanalytic hypotheses. This sense of inadequacy, and the despair that goes with it, may in some cases at least translate into abandonment of scientific for hermeneutic goals.

3. There are those, inside and outside psychoanalysis, who insist that work in the neural sciences is capable of falsifying or casting doubt upon psychoanalytic hypotheses, and in fact that it does or will do so.

What is needed in order to cope with these circumstances?

First, just what sort of entity psychoanalytic theory is must be clarified. The new nonstatement view of theory promises to be useful in any attempt to systematize and explicate psychoanalytic concepts and hypotheses, decide what the domains of application of psychoanalysis are, and think through what the relation between neural science and psychoanalysis is. The nonstatement view of theory casts as well some light on the attitude (judged harshly by some) of psychoanalysts who hold psychoanalytic theory to be useful, even in the face of instances of failure to obtain adequate inductive support for some of its propositions.

Second, psychoanalysis should prepare itself to exploit recent conceptual and methodological developments in single subject research, in order to argue more cogently questions about validity and generalizability in its single case studies.

Third, psychoanalysis should not turn its back on the theory of probability. When, as has been recently proposed, probability is interpreted as an objective propensity of a single case, it is especially suitable for use in single case studies. Many psychoanalytic hypotheses might be better formulated probabilistically. Statistical reasoning is a powerful conceptual tool, even in single subject research, for arguing a relation between hypothesis and evidence.

At this time, what should be the response to the challenge of eliminative inductivism, especially when it is expressed in the provocative conclusion that psychoanalytic hypotheses cannot be tested in the psychoanalytic situation? Psychoanalysis may want especially to consider proceeding according to the following recommendations, if its response is to be "Yes, psychoanalytic hypotheses CAN BE tested in the psychoanalytic situation."

1. Seek falsifications rather than confirmations in case studies.

2. Adopt the strategy of carrying out a number of independent and different kinds of studies to test a particular hypothesis, and, in each such study (making use in some of quasi-experimental designs for single subject research), attempt to eliminate at least one—and in each case a different—alternative explanation of an outcome apparently credibilifying that hypothesis.

3. Use causal modeling and statistical controls in order to be able to argue that a causal relation holds when data are—as in single subject studies they often are—nonexperimental rather than experimental.

4. Make a careful decision about what data are considered in a psychoanalytic study to be indisputably nontheoretical data, and distinguish nontheoretical data statements (about facts) sharply from hypotheses to be tested.

5. To cope with the putative role of suggestion as a plausible alternative explanatory candidate, which might be supposed to account for an outcome apparently supporting a psychoanalytic hypothesis:

*a*) Minimize suggestion through a disciplined use of psychoanalytic technique.

*b*) Predict responses by the analysand to an interpretation that have not previously been manifested and that are not suggested by that interpretation.

*c*) Consider what relatively suggestion-resistant performances of the analysand might be used as relevant data.

*d*) Most of all, study the contexts of acts of interpretation to measure whether, how, and to what extent the psychoanalyst is conveying unwittingly verbal and nonverbal cues to the analysand, and whether, how, and to what extent the analysand interprets such cues as expressing expectations for certain responses and not others.

6. To cope with the putative liabilities of data obtained from free association:

*a*) Make explicit the prior criteria governing the psychoanalyst's selection among associations (and study the extent to which in a particular case the psychoanalyst adheres to or departs from these).

*b*) Make explicit the basis for the psychoanalyst's distinction between the quality of different data with respect to contamination by influences which might provide plausible alternative explanations for the occurrence of an outcome apparently supporting a psychoanalytic hypothesis.

*c*) Make explicit the assumptions about the mind presupposed by the method of free association, and provide evidential justification for accepting these that is independent of the method.

*d*) Study ways of identifying and distinguishing between reality-accommodative and constructive aspects of memory.

7. To cope with questions about the use of therapeutic outcomes as evidential support for psychoanalytic hypotheses (when these hypotheses have been used in making the interpretations that are regarded as necessary to bring about these outcomes):

*a*) Make explicit the nature of the actual outcomes sought by psychoanalysis as treatment, and distinguish such outcomes from those of other treatment modalities.

*b*) Devise means of detecting and demonstrating (probably in the psychoanalytic situation) changes in an analysand's dispositions or propensities rather than merely changes in his behavior.

*c*) Specify what in addition to veridical insight through interpretation is necessary to achieve these therapeutic outcomes.

8. Build upon Luborsky's symptom-context method, and Glymour's bootstrap strategy for testing theories, both consistent with the canons of eliminative inductivism, in carrying out and analyzing data from single subject studies.

9. Explicate the centrality of the reappearance in the transference— of the presence in the here-and-now of the psychoanalytic situation—of

pathogenic factors and their effects for any attempt, using clinical data as evidence, to demonstrate, for example, the causal relevance of conflict and defense to the formation, change in severity or frequency, or remission of neurotic symptoms.

Certainly, in any attempt to proceed according to such recommendations, the demands upon psychoanalysis will be great. A research program—a set of formidable theoretical, methodological, and substantive problems for psychoanalytic investigators to solve—is implied once the necessity for satisfying the canons of eliminative inductivism is accepted. But how can one not accept this necessity? Eliminative inductivism is not some artificial prescription of logicians. It is another name for scientific reasoning, which found one familiar expression in the writings of John Stuart Mill, and which has proved itself as a means for testing our beliefs about the world. Considering the implications of ignoring persistent, troublesome, and well-reasoned questions about the scientific status of psychoanalysis, I do not see any alternative for a new generation of psychoanalytic investigators except to bestir itself to carry out the needed work. That is just one of the responsibilities that goes with being a psychoanalyst.

# Technical Notes

1. The logical form of a definition of a theoretical predicate $P$ is: $X$ is a $P$ if and only if $T$. The symbol $X$ is to be replaced by the name of a particular domain or system. The symbol $P$ is to be replaced by a predicate which can be used to describe a domain or system as a certain kind of domain or system. The symbol $T$ is to be replaced by conditions which must be satisfied if the predicate is to be true of the domain or system described by it.

2. A theoretical predicate, which is a linguistic entity, is true of a domain if and only if the domain satisfies the condition $T$. The condition $T$ which must be satisfied can be expressed in a variety of languages. Among these languages are: ($a$) first-order predicate logic with identity, ($b$) set theory, ($c$) mathematical equations interpreted in terms of causal relations between or among measurable variables.

$a$) A domain $X$ is a set of individuals and their properties or the relations between or among them. $T$ is a set of abstract axiomatic formulae, stated in the language of first-order predicate logic with identity. A domain interprets these abstract axiomatic formulae if every individual constant ($a$, $b$, $c$, . . . ) in these formulae can be assigned to an individual in the domain, and every predicate ($A^1$, $B^1$, $C^1$ . . . , $A^2$, $B^2$, $C^2$, . . . , $A^3$, $B^3$, $C^3$, . . . , $A^n$, $B^n$, $C^n$ . . . ) in these formulae can be assigned, respectively, to a monadic relation (a property, which can be exemplified by single individuals in the domain); a diadic relation (exemplified by ordered pairs of individuals); a triadic relation (exemplified by ordered triads of individuals); or an $n$-adic relation (exemplified by ordered $n$-ads of individuals). The domain $X$ satisfies $T$ or is a model of $T$ if and only if, when $X$ is an interpretation of $T$, each abstract axiomatic formula becomes a statement (an axiom or theorem) which is true of $X$. (See, for example, Mates [1972] and Tarski [1941]. There are difficulties in formulating the axioms of most sciences in the language of first-order predicate logic with identity.)

$b$) A domain $X$ is a set-theoretic structure—an ordered set of sets and relations (including operations and functions). $T$ is a set of abstract axioms. These state, in the language of set theory, what kinds of relations or functions obtain within and between particular sets. The domain is a particular kind of set-theoretic structure if and only if $X$ satisfies or is a model of $T$ (if and only if $X$ is an interpretation of $T$ which makes the abstract axioms true statements about $X$). (See Suppes, 1957, 1967.)

$c$) $T$ is a set of laws, or hypotheses about deterministic or probabilistic relations between or among nontheoretic and theoretic variables. These relations may be but are not necessarily expressed in the language of mathematical equations. A domain $X$ satisfies $T$ just in case these laws or hypotheses are true of $X$.

3. To identify a particular psychological entity, a scientist must be able to characterize it in terms of a particular state of affairs, and must also be able to assign it to an attitude-set (the kind of attitude the subject producing the psychological entity has toward the state of affairs). A scientist, therefore, will represent a particular psychological entity as an ordered set with three members: a subject, an attitude, and a state of affairs. The state of affairs may be designated by a sentence (or an inscription of a sentence)—or by a predicate, designating a relation (one constituent of the state of affairs), and the names or descriptions of entities to which this predicate applies (other constituents of the state of affairs). Such a sentence for the subject gives the minimal conditions a particular state of affairs must satisfy to be the state of affairs he believes, wishes, perceives. So one may consider a sentence, which for the believing, wishing, perceiving subject designates or describes a state of affairs, an individuating property of a psychological entity.

Thus, where $x$ is a linguistic variable taking psychological entities as values, and John's belief that Jack loves Jane is a psychological entity, one may write

 *a*) $J_i\,x$

 *b*) Bx

 *c*) ("That Jack loves Jane")$x$ as a way of saying, first, that a psychological entity $x$ is a $J_i$—is a member of the domain comprised by the psychological entities produced by the subject John, and is also a member of a psychological state $i$ (a superset of coexisting or concurrent sets of attitudes of one subject), a subset of the John-domain; second, that a psychological entity $x$ is a B—is a member of a set of beliefs, a subset of the psychological state $i$; and, third, that a psychological entity $x$ is a "That Jack loves Jane" type or kind of psychological entity, or a "That Jack loves Jane" way of representing for the subject John a particular state of affairs. The latter characterization of a psychological entity implies that John believes that the sentence "Jack loves Jane" is true, or believes that a "Jack loves Jane" type or kind of state of affairs obtains in the actual world.

Similarly, to represent John's belief that Mary wishes that Joe loved her, one may say that:

 *a*) $x$ is a member of the domain of the psychological entities produced by the subject John in a psychological state $i$.

 *b*) $x$ is a belief.

 *c*) $x$ is a "That Joe loves Mary is Mary's wish" type or kind of psychological entity.

A more complicated formulation of $c$ is:

 *c*) $x$ is a ["That $y$ is a member of the domain comprised by the psychological entities produced by some subject Mary, and also a member of the psychological state $k$, which is a subset of the Mary-domain & That $y$ is a wish & That $y$ is a 'Joe loves Mary' type or kind of psychological entity"] type or kind of psychological entity. (Such a formulation makes clear in just what way the use of the language of first-order predicate logic to express the propositions of science may be infelicitous.)

4. A state of affairs is a sequence of elements, which are its constituents: a property (an attribute or "monadic relation") or in general any $n$-adic relation (monadic, diadic, triadic . . . , $n$-adic), and an entity or ordered set of entities exemplifying the property or relation.

5. Suppose that some theory has variables $A$, $B$, $C$, $D$, $E$, $F$, and $G$. The variables $A$ and $D$ are theoretic. The variables $B$ and $E$ are nontheoretic. The variable $A$ is related to the variable $B$; the relation is given, say, by the hypothesis $A = f_1(B)$, where the function

$f_1$ expresses the nature of the relation between $A$ and $B$. The function $f_1$ may describe a procedure whereby, knowing the value of the variable $B$, one can calculate the value of the variable $A$. So, if the function $f_1$ is the instruction "square $B$ to get $A$," we have the "law" $A = B^2$. Similarly, in the same theory, the variable $A$ may be related in turn to the variable $D$ by the function $f_2$, the variable $C$ to the variable $F$ by the function $f_3$, the variable $E$ to the variable $D$ by the function $f_4$, and the variable $F$ to the variable $G$ by the function $f_5$. These relations may be given by the hypotheses: $A = f_2(D)$, $C = f_3(F)$, $E = f_4(D)$, and $F = f_5(G)$.

So, if $A = B^2$, $A = 5D$, and $E = 2D$, and $B = 25$ is observed empirically, the theory leads us to predict: from $A = B^2$, that the theoretic variable $A = 525$; from $A = 5D$, that the theoretic variable $D = 105$; and from the value of the theoretic variable $D$, that the nontheoretic variable $E = 210$. If $E$ is discovered empirically to be 210, the three hypotheses are regarded as having escaped disconfirmation and having achieved through the convergence of predictions some degree of support. If $E$ is discovered to be other than 210, one of the three hypotheses (we cannot know from this one "experiment" alone just which one) is false, and the three hypotheses together are disconfirmed. The hypotheses $C = f_3(F)$ and $F = f_5(G)$, which are part of the theory, have not been tested at all by this "experiment."

# References

Achen, C. 1982. *Interpreting and Using Regression*. Beverly Hills, Calif.: Sage.

Arlow, J., & Brenner, C. 1964. *Psychoanalytic Concepts and the Structural Theory*. New York: International Universities Press.

Arnold, M., ed. 1970. *Feelings and Emotions*. New York: Academic Press.

Asher, H. 1976. *Causal Modeling*. Beverly Hills, Calif.: Sage.

Barwise, J., & Perry, J. 1981. Semantic innocence and uncompromising situations. In *The Foundations of Analytic Philosophy*, eds. P. French et al., pp. 387–404. Minneapolis: University of Minnesota Press.

Blalock, H. 1961. *Causal Inferences in Nonexperimental Research*. New York: W. W. Norton, 1972.

———. 1969. *Theory Construction*. Englewood Cliffs, N.J.: Prentice-Hall.

Bolgar, H. 1965. The case study method. In *Handbook of Clinical Psychology*, ed. B. Wolman, pp. 28–39. New York: McGraw-Hill.

Breuer, J., & Freud, S. 1893–1895. Studies on hysteria. *S.E.*, 2.

Brown, H. 1977. *Perception, Theory and Commitment*. Chicago: University of Chicago Press.

Buchler, J., ed. 1940. *Philosophical Writings of Peirce*. New York: Dover, 1955.

Bunge, M. 1979. *Causality and Modern Science*. 3d ed., rev. New York: Dover.

Campbell, D., & Stanley, J. 1963. *Experimental and Quasi-Experimental Designs for Research*. Chicago: Rand McNally.

Carnap, R. 1936a. Testability and meaning I. *Philosophy of Science*, 3:420–471.

———. 1936b. Testability and meaning II. *Philosophy of Science*, 4: 1–40.

———. 1956. *Meaning and Necessity*. Enl. ed. Chicago: University of Chicago Press, 1958.

———. 1958. *Introduction to Symbolic Logic and Its Applications*. New York: Dover.

NOTE: *S.E.* = *The Standard Edition of the Complete Psychological Works of Sigmund Freud* (London: Hogarth Press).

Chassan, J. 1953. The role of statistics in psychoanalysis. *Psychiatry*, 16:153–165.

———. 1956. On probability theory and psychoanalytic research. *Psychiatry*, 19:55–61.

———. 1960. Statistical inference and the single case in clinical design. *Psychiatry*, 23:173–184.

———. 1961. Stochastic models of the single case as the basis of clinical research design. *Behavioral Science*, 6:42–50.

———. 1962. Probability processes in psychoanalytic psychiatry. In *Theories of the Mind*, ed. J. Scher, pp. 598–618. New York: Free Press.

———. 1970. On psychodynamics and clinical research methodology. *Psychiatry*, 33:94–101.

———. 1979. *Research Design in Clinical Psychology and Psychiatry*. 2d ed., enl., New York: Irvington.

Chomsky, N. 1957. *Syntactic Structures*. The Hague: Mouton.

———. 1972. *Language and Mind*. New York: Harcourt Brace Jovanovich.

Cook, T., & Campbell, D. 1976. The design and conduct of quasi-experiments and true experiments in field settings. In *Handbook of Industrial and Organizational Psychology*, ed. M. Dunnette, pp. 223–326. Chicago: Rand McNally.

———. 1979. *Quasi-Experimentation*. Boston: Houghton Mifflin.

Danto, A. 1959. Meaning and theoretical terms in psychoanalysis. In Hook (1959), pp. 314–318.

Davidson, D. 1967a. The logical form of action sentences. In Davidson and Harman (1975), pp. 235–246.

———. 1967b. Causal relations. In Davidson and Harman (1975), pp. 247–254.

———. 1968–1969. On saying that. In Davidson and Harman (1975), pp. 143–152.

Davidson, D., & Harman, G., eds. 1975. *The Logic of Grammar*. Encino, Calif.: Dickenson.

Davidson, P., & Costello, C., eds. 1969. *N = 1: Experimental Studies of Single Cases*. New York: Van Nostrand Reinhold.

Davitz, J. 1970. A dictionary and grammar of emotion. In Arnold (1970), pp. 251–258.

Dennett, D. 1978. *Brainstorms*. Montgomery, Vt.: Bradford Books.

Dukes, W. 1965. N = 1. *Psychological Bulletin*, 64:74–79.

Edelson, J. 1983. Freud's use of metaphor. *Psychoanalytic Study of the Child*, eds. A. Solnit et al., 38:17–59. New Haven: Yale University Press.

Edelson, M. 1954. *The Science of Psychology and the Concept of Energy*. Ph.D. diss., Department of Psychology, University of Chicago.

————. 1971. *The Idea of a Mental Illness*. New Haven: Yale University Press.

————. 1972. Language and dreams. *Psychoanalytic Study of the Child*, eds. R. Eissler et al., 27:203–282. New York: Quadrangle Books.

————. 1975. *Language and Interpretation in Psychoanalysis*. New Haven: Yale University Press.

————. 1976. Toward a study of interpretation in psychoanalysis. In *Explorations in General Theory in Social Science*, eds. J. Loubser et al., 151–181. New York: Free Press.

————. 1977. Psychoanalysis as science. *Journal of Nervous and Mental Disease*, 165:1–28.

————. 1978. What is the psychoanalyst talking about? In *Psychoanalysis and Language*, ed. J. Smith, pp. 99–170. New Haven: Yale University Press.

Edelson, M., & Jones, A. 1954. Operational exploration of the conceptual self system and of the interaction between frames of reference. *Genetic Psychology Monographs*, 50:43–139.

Edgington, E. 1967. Statistical inference from N = 1 experiments. *Journal of Psychology*, 65:195–199.

————. 1972. The design of one-subject experiments for testing hypotheses. *Western Psychologist*, 3:33–38.

————. 1980a. Validity of randomization tests for one-subject experiments. *Journal of Educational Statistics*, 5:235–251.

————. 1980b. Overcoming obstacles to single-subject experimentation. *Journal of Educational Statistics*, 5:261–267.

————. 1980c. *Randomization Tests*. New York: Marcel Dekker.

Ezriel, H. 1956. Experimentation within the psycho-analytic session I. *British Journal for the Philosophy of Science*, 7:29–48.

————. 1957. Experimentation within the psycho-analytic session II. *British Journal for the Philosophy of Science*, 7:342–347.

Federn, P. 1952. *Ego Psychology and the Psychoses*. New York: Basic Books.

Feibleman, J. 1946. *An Introduction to the Philosophy of Charles S. Peirce*. Cambridge, Mass: MIT, 1970.

Feinstein, A. 1977. *Clinical Biostatistics*. St. Louis: C. V. Mosby.

Fenichel, O. 1935. Concerning the theory of psychoanalytic technique. In *The Collected Papers of Otto Fenichel: First Series*, pp. 332–348. New York: W. W. Norton, 1953.

————. 1941. *Problems of Psychoanalytic Technique*. New York: Psychoanalytic Quarterly.

————. 1945. *The Psychoanalytic Theory of Neurosis*. New York: W. W. Norton.

Freeman, L. 1965. *Elementary Applied Statistics*. New York: Wiley.

Freud, S. 1900. The interpretation of dreams. *S.E.*, 4 & 5.

————. 1911. Psychoanalytic notes on an autobiographical account of a case of paranoia. *S.E.*, 12:9–82.

————. 1915. Instincts and their vicissitudes. *S.E.*, 14:117–140.

————. 1916–1917. Introductory lectures on psycho-analysis. *S.E.*, 15 & 16.

————. 1937. Constructions in analysis. *S.E.*, 23:257–269.

Giere, R. 1973. Objective single-case probabilities and the foundations of statistics. In *Logic, Methodology and Philosophy of Science IV*, eds. P. Suppes et al., pp. 467–483. Amsterdam: North-Holland.

————. 1979a. Foundations of probability and statistical inference. In *Current Research in Philosophy of Science*, eds. P. Asquith & H. Kyburg, pp. 503–533. East Lansing, Mich.: Philosophy of Science Association.

————. 1979b. *Understanding Scientific Reasoning*. New York: Holt, Rinehart & Winston.

————. 1980. Causal systems and statistical hypotheses. In *Applications of Inductive Logic*, eds. L. Cohen & M. Hesse, pp. 251–270. Oxford: Clarendon Press.

Gill, M. 1963. Topography and systems in psychoanalytic theory. *Psychological Issues*. Monograph 10. New York: International Universities Press.

————. 1982. *Analysis of Transference*. Vol. 1. *Theory and Technique*. *Psychological Issues*. Monograph 53. New York: International Universities Press.

Gill, M., & Hoffman, I. 1982. A method for studying the analysis of aspects of the patient's experience of the relationship in psychoanalysis and psychotherapy. *Journal of the American Psychoanalytic Association*, 30:137–167.

Glymour, C. 1974. Freud, Kepler, and the clinical evidence. In *Freud*, ed. R. Wollheim, pp. 285–304. Garden City, N.Y.: Anchor.

————. 1980. *Theory and Evidence*. Princeton, N.J.: Princeton University Press.

Gottman, J. 1973. N-of-one and N-of-two research in psychotherapy. *Psychological Bulletin*, 80:93–105.

Group for the Advancement of Psychiatry. 1959. Some observations on controls in psychiatric research. *Report Number 42*. New York: GAP Publications Office.

Grünbaum, A. 1977a. How scientific is psychoanalysis? In *Science and Psychotherapy*, eds. R. Stern et al., pp. 219–254. New York: Haven.

————. 1977b. Is psychoanalysis a pseudo-science? I. *Zeitschrift für philosophische Forschung*, 31:333–353.

————. 1978. Is psychoanalysis a pseudo-science? II. *Zeitschrift für philosophische Forschung*, 32:49–69.

————. 1979. Is Freudian psychoanalytic theory pseudo-scientific by

Karl Popper's criterion of demarcation? *American Philosophical Quarterly*, 16:131–141.

———. 1980. Epistemological liabilities of the clinical appraisal of psychoanalytic theory. *Noûs*, 14:307–385.

———. 1981. The placebo concept. *Behavior Research and Therapy*, 19:157–167.

———. 1982a. Logical foundations of psychoanalytic theory. In Festschrift for Wolfgang Stegmüller, eds. W. Essler & H. Putnam. Boston: D. Reidel. In press.

———. 1982b. Can psychoanalytic theory be cogently tested "on the couch"? Parts I & II. *Psychoanalysis and Contemporary Thought*, 5:155–255, 311–436.

Hacking, I. 1965. *Logic of Statistical Inference*. Cambridge: Cambridge University Press.

Hanson, N. 1958. *Patterns of Discovery*. London: Cambridge University Press, 1965.

Hartmann, H. 1958. *Ego Psychology and the Problem of Adaptation*. New York: International Universities Press.

———. 1959. Psychoanalysis as a scientific theory. In Hook (1959), pp. 3–37.

Hays, W. 1973. *Statistics for the Social Sciences*. 2d ed. New York: Holt, Rinehart & Winston.

Hempel, C. 1965. *Aspects of Scientific Explanation*. New York: Free Press.

Herbst, P. 1970. *Behavioural Worlds*. London: Tavistock.

Hersen, M., & Barlow, D. 1976. *Single-Case Experimental Designs*. New York: Pergamon Press.

Hildebrand, D; Laing, J.; & Rosenthal, H. 1977. *Prediction Analysis of Cross Classifications*. New York: Wiley.

Hobson, J., & McCarley, R. 1977. The brain as a dream state generator. *American Journal of Psychiatry*, 134:1335–1348.

Hook, S., ed. 1959. *Psychoanalysis, Scientific Method and Philosophy*. New York: Grove Press, 1960.

Hospers, J. 1959. Philosophy and psychoanalysis. In Hook (1959), pp. 336–357.

Kaplan, D. 1968. Quantifying in. In Davidson and Harman (1975), pp. 160–181.

Karasu, T., et al. 1982. *Psychotherapy Research: Methodological and Efficacy Issues*. New York: American Psychiatric Association.

Kazdin, A. 1976. Statistical analyses for single-case experimental designs. In Hersen and Barlow (1976), pp. 265–316.

———. 1980a. *Research Design in Clinical Psychology*. New York: Harper & Row.

———. 1980b. Obstacles in using randomization tests in single-case experimentation. *Journal of Educational Statistics*, 5:253–260.

———. 1981. Drawing valid inferences from case studies. *Journal of Consulting and Clinical Psychology*, 49:183–192.

———. 1982. Single-case experimental designs. In *Handbook of Research Methods in Clinical Psychology*, eds. P. Kendall & J. Butcher, pp. 461–490. New York: Wiley.

Klein, G. 1976. *Psychoanalytic Theory*. New York: International Universities Press.

Kohut, H. 1979. The two analyses of Mr. Z. *International Journal of Psycho-Analysis*, 60:3–27.

Kratochwill, T. 1978. *Single Subject Research*. New York: Academic Press.

Kris, A. 1982. *Free Association*. New Haven: Yale University Press.

Kris, E. 1956a. On some vicissitudes of insight in psycho-analysis. *International Journal of Psycho-Analysis*, 37:445–455.

———. 1956b. The recovery of childhood memories in psychoanalysis. *Psychoanalytic Study of the Child*, eds. R. Eissler et al., 11:54–88. New York: International Universities Press.

Kuhn, T. 1970. *The Structure of Scientific Revolutions*. 2d ed. Chicago: University of Chicago Press.

Kyburg, H. 1970. *Probability and Inductive Logic*. New York: Macmillan.

Leach, C. 1979. *Introduction to Statistics*. New York: Wiley.

Leeper, R. 1970. The motivational and perceptual properties of emotions as indicating their fundamental character and role. In Arnold (1970), pp. 151–168.

Leitenberg, H. 1973. The use of single-case methodology in psychotherapy research. *Journal of Abnormal Psychology*, 82:87–101.

Loewenstein, R. 1957. Some thoughts on interpretation in the theory and practice of psychoanalysis. *Psychoanalytic Study of the Child*, eds. R. Eissler et al., 12:127–150. New York: International Universities Press.

Luborsky, L. 1967. Momentary forgetting during psychotherapy and psychoanalysis. In *Motives and Thought*, ed. R. Holt, pp. 177–217. *Psychological Issues*. Monograph 18/19. New York: International Universities Press.

———. 1973. Forgetting and remembering (momentary forgetting) during psychotherapy. In *Psychoanalytic Research*, ed. M. Mayman, pp. 29–55. *Psychological Issues*. Monograph 30. New York: International Universities Press.

Luborsky, L. & Mintz, J. 1974. What sets off momentary forgetting during a psychoanalysis? *Psychoanalysis and Contemporary Science*, 3:233–268.

Luborsky, L., & Spence, D. 1978. Quantitative research on psychoanalytic therapy. In *Handbook of Psychotherapy and Behavior Change*, eds. S. Garfield & A. Bergin, pp. 331–368. New York: Wiley.

Luborsky, L., et al. 1979. Preconditions and consequences of transference interpretations: a clinical-quantitative investigation. *Journal of Nervous and Mental Disease*, 167:391–401.

McCarley, R., & Hobson, J. 1977. The neurobiological origins of psychoanalytic dream theory. *American Journal of Psychiatry*, 134: 1211–1221.

Malan, D. H. 1976. *The Frontier of Brief Psychotherapy*. New York: Plenum.

———. 1979. *Individual Psychotherapy and the Science of Psychodynamics*. Boston: Butterworths.

Marcus, R. 1981. A proposed solution to a puzzle about belief. In *The Foundations of Analytic Philosophy*, eds. P. French et al., pp. 501–510. Minneapolis: University of Minnesota Press.

Mates, B. 1972. *Elementary Logic*. New York: Oxford University Press.

Mellor, D. 1971. *The Matter of Chance*. Cambridge: Cambridge University Press.

Miller, G.; Galanter, E.; & Pribram, K. 1960. *Plans and the Structure of Behavior*. New York: Holt, Rinehart & Winston.

Nagel, E. 1939. *Principles of the Theory of Probability*. Chicago: University of Chicago Press.

———. 1959. Methodological issues in psychoanalytic theory. In Hook (1959), pp. 38–56.

Osgood, C.; Suci, G.; & Tannenbaum, P. 1957. *The Measurement of Meaning*. Urbana: University of Illinois Press.

Pap, A. 1959. On the empirical interpretation of psychoanalytic concepts. In Hook (1959), pp. 283–297.

Paul, L., ed. 1963a. *Psychoanalytic Clinical Interpretation*. New York: Free Press.

———. 1963b. The logic of psychoanalytic interpretation. In Paul (1963a), pp. 249–272.

Peters, R. 1970. The education of the emotions. In Arnold (1970), pp. 187–203.

Platt, J. 1964. Strong inference. *Science*, 146:347–353.

Popper, K. 1959a. *The Logic of Scientific Discovery*. Rev. ed. New York: Harper & Row, 1968.

———. 1959b. The propensity interpretation of probability. *British Journal for the Philosophy of Science*, 10:25–42.

———. 1963. *Conjectures and Refutations*. London: Routledge & Kegan Paul.

Pribram, K. 1970. Feelings as monitors. In Arnold (1970), pp. 41–53.

———. 1971. *Languages of the Brain*. Englewood Cliffs, N.J.: Prentice-Hall.

Quine, W. 1953. Three grades of modal involvement. In *The Ways of Paradox*, pp. 158–176. Rev. and enl. ed. Cambridge: Harvard University Press, 1976.

———. 1955. Quantifiers and propositional attitudes. In *The Ways of Paradox*, pp. 185–196. Rev. and enl. ed. Cambridge: Harvard University Press, 1976.

———. 1970. *Philosophy of Logic*. Englewood Cliff, N.J.: Prentice-Hall.

———. 1979. Intensions revisited. In *Contemporary Perspectives in the Philosophy of Language*, eds. P. French et al., pp. 268–274. Minneapolis: University of Minnesota Press.

Railton, P. 1978. A deductive-nomological model of probabilistic explanation. *Philosophy of Science*, 45:206–226.

Rapaport, D. 1950. On the psychoanalytic theory of thinking. In *Collected Papers of David Rapaport*, ed M. Gill. pp. 313–328. New York: Basic Books, 1967.

———. 1951. The conceptual model of psychoanalysis. In *Collected Papers of David Rapaport*, ed. M. Gill, pp. 405–431. New York: Basic Books, 1967.

———. 1953. On the psychoanalytic theory of affects. In *Collected Papers of David Rapaport*, ed. M. Gill, pp. 476–512. New York: Basic Books, 1967.

———. (with M. Gill) 1959a. The points of view and assumptions of metapsychology. In *Collected Papers of David Rapaport*, ed. M. Gill, pp. 795–811. New York: Basic Books, 1967.

———. 1959b. The structure of psychoanalytic theory. *Psychological Issues*, Monograph 6, 1960.

———. 1960. On the psychoanalytic theory of motivation. In *Collected Papers of David Rapaport*, ed. M. Gill, pp. 853–915. New York: Basic Books, 1967.

Reichenbach, H. 1947. *Elements of Symbolic Logic*. New York: Free Press, 1966.

Reiser, M. 1975. Changing theoretical concepts in psychosomatic medicine. In *American Handbook of Psychiatry*, vol. 4, ed. M. Reiser, pp. 477–500. 2d ed. New York: Basic Books.

Robinson, P., & Foster, D. 1979. *Experimental Psychology: A Small-N Approach*. New York: Harper & Row.

Rozeboom, W. 1961. Ontological induction and the logical typology of scientific variables. *Philosophy of Science*, 28:337–377.

Rubinstein, B. 1967. Explanation and mere description: a metascientific examination of certain aspects of the psychoanalytic theory of motivation. In *Motives and Thought*, ed. R. Holt, pp. 18–77. *Psychological Issues*, Monograph 18/19. New York: International Universities Press.

————. 1974. On the role of classificatory processes in mental functioning. *Psychoanalysis and Contemporary Science*, 3:101–185.

————. 1975. On the clinical psychoanalytic theory and its role in the inference and confirmation of particular clinical hypotheses. *Psychoanalysis and Contemporary Science*, 4:3–57.

————. 1976. On the possibility of a strictly clinical psychoanalytic theory. In *Psychology versus Metapsychology*, eds. M. Gill & P. Holzman, pp. 229–264. *Psychological Issues*, Monograph 36. New York: International Universities Press.

Salmon, W. 1959. Psychoanalytical theory and evidence. In Hook (1959), pp. 252–267.

————. 1966. *The Foundations of Scientific Inference*. Pittsburgh: University of Pittsburgh Press.

————. 1970. Statistical explanation. In *Statistical Explanation and Statistical Relevance*, pp. 29–87. Pittsburgh: University of Pittsburgh Press, 1971.

Scheffler, I. 1963. *The Anatomy of Inquiry*. New York: Knopf.

Schur, M. 1966. *The Id and the Regulatory Principles of Mental Functioning*. New York: International Universities Press.

Searl, M. 1936. Some queries on principles of technique. *International Journal of Psychoanalysis*, 17:471–493.

Shapiro, M. 1961. A method of measuring psychological changes specific to the individual psychiatric patient. *British Journal of Medical Psychology*, 34:151–155.

————. 1963. A clinical approach to fundamental research with special reference to the study of the single patient. In *Methods of Psychiatric Research*, eds. P. Sainsbury N. Kreitman, pp. 123–149. New York: Oxford University Press.

————. 1966. The single case in clinical-psychological research. *Journal of General Psychology*, 74:3–23.

Shontz, F. 1965. *Research Methods in Personality*. New York: Appleton-Century-Crofts.

Sidman, M. 1960. *Tactics of Scientific Research*. New York: Basic Books.

Siegel, S. 1956. *Nonparametric Statistics for the Behavioral Sciences*. New York: McGraw-Hill.

Skyrms, B. 1975. *Choice and Chance*. Encino, Calif.: Dickenson.

Spence, D. 1982. *Narrative Truth and Historical Truth*. New York: W. W. Norton.

Stegmüller, W. 1976. *The Structure and Dynamics of Theories*. New York: Springer-Verlag.

Stephenson, W. 1953. *The Study of Behavior*. Chicago: University of Chicago Press.

————. 1974. Methodology of single case studies. *Journal of Operational Psychiatry*, 5:3–16.

Stone, L. 1961. *The Psychoanalytic Situation*. New York: International Universities Press.

Strachey, J. 1934. The nature of the therapeutic action of psycho-analysis. *International Journal of Psycho-Analysis*, 15:127–159.

Suppe, F. 1977. *The Structure of Scientific Theories*. 2d ed. Urbana: University of Illinois Press.

Suppes, P. 1957. *Introduction to Logic*. New York: D. Van Nostrand.

————. 1967. What is a scientific theory? In *Philosophy of Science Today*, ed. S. Morgenbesser, pp. 55–67. New York: Basic Books.

————. 1970. *A Probabilistic Theory of Causality*. Amsterdam: North-Holland.

Tarski, A. 1941. *Introduction to Logic*. New York: Oxford University Press.

————. 1944. The semantic conception of truth. In *Semantics and the Philosophy of Language*, ed. L. Linsky, pp. 13–17. Urbana: University of Illinois Press, 1952.

————. 1969. Truth and proof. *Scientific American*, 220:63–77.

Taylor, B. 1976. States of affairs. In *Truth and Meaning*, eds. G. Evans & J. McDowell, pp. 263–284. Oxford: Clarendon Press.

Van Fraassen, B. 1972. A formal approach to the philosophy of science. In *Paradigms and Paradoxes*, ed. R. Colodny, pp. 303–366. Pittsburgh: University of Pittsburg Press.

Vendler, Z. 1967. Causal relations. In Davidson and Harman (1975), pp. 255–261.

Waelder, R. 1960. *Basic Theory of Psychoanalysis*. New York: International Universities Press.

Watson, G., & McGaw, D. 1980. *Statistical Inquiry*. New York: Wiley.

White, A. 1970. *Truth*. New York: Anchor Books.

Wiener, P., ed. 1958. *Charles S. Peirce: Selected Writings*. New York: Dover, 1966.

Wisdom, J. 1956. Psycho-analytic technology. *British Journal for the Philosophy of Science*, 7:13–28.

————. 1967. Testing an interpretation within a session. *International Journal of Psycho-Analysis*, 48:44–52.

Wollheim, R. 1979. Wish-fulfillment. In *Rational Action*, ed. R. Harrison, pp. 47–60. New York: Cambridge University Press.

# Index

Achen, C., 153
Alternative hypotheses, 4–5, 28–30, 42–43, 45–46, 64–65, 68, 125–27; in psychoanalysis, 51–53, 61–62. *See also* Bias; Control of relevant variables
Arlow, J., 79
Arnold, M., 89n.6
Asher, H., 124
Auxiliary assumptions, 23, 28, 36. *See also* Testing hypotheses

Barlow, D., 67, 124
Barwise, J., 91n.11
Bias, 23; introduced by analysand's preconceptions, 46, 53, 136–37; selection, of psychoanalyst, 46, 53, 134–37. *See also* Alternative hypotheses
Blalock, H., 124
Bolgar, H., 61
Brenner, C., 79
Breuer, J., xiv, 50, 67
Brown, H., 9n, 12n.6
Buchler, J., 91n.12
Bunge, M., 123

Campbell, D., 5n.2, 59, 64, 67–68, 124, 125, 126–27
Canons, scientific, xi–xii, 5; for single subject research, 3. *See also* Eliminative inductivism, canons of
Carnap, R., 12n.6, 24n, 120
Case: of Anna O., xiv, 50, 67, 124, 134, 150; of Miss X, xiv, 144–47; of Mr. Z, xiv, 61–62; of Rat Man, xiv, 3, 40, 48, 60, 121, 144, 147–50
Chassan, J., 63, 74

Chomsky, N., 8, 21n.4, 116
Comparative support, premise of, 42–43, 45
Confirmation, 1, 4, 7–16, 36, 43; and nonstatement view of theory, 13; and psychoanalytic theory, 15–16; versus falsification, 22. *See also* Logical positivism; Verification
Context of discovery or justification. *See* Falsificationism, and context of discovery or justification
Control of relevant variables, 59–60, 125–26. *See also* Alternative hypotheses
Cook, T., 5n.2, 124, 125, 126–27
Coordinating definition, 9, 10, 11, 15
Correspondence rule. *See* Coordinating definition
Correspondence theory. *See* Truth
Corroboration, 27
Costello, C., 61
Counterexample, 15–16, 23, 39n, 144
Credibility, scientific, 2, 42; of psychoanalytic hypotheses, 4–5, 46–47, 62–63. *See also* Eliminative inductivism

Danto, A., 13, 14
Data: probative, 4, 43; obtained in the psychoanalytic situation, 41, 52–54; theory-free or theory-laden, 19–20, 129; underdetermination of hypotheses by, 2, 20, 35, 36. *See also* Observation language
Davidson, D., 87n.5, 91n.9
Davidson, P., 61
Davitz, J., 89n.6
Dennett, D., 115, 116, 118